WHERE WERE YOU?

I'VE BEEN WAITING FOR YOU!

MARIE-MADELEINE KABANGE NGOIE
ALAIN AVANTHEY

Biography

Mary Magdalene at 72 years old
© 2024 Alain Avanthey

Thank you to Reverend Mylene Muswamba Mudiay Bila and Microsoft Translator.

Thank you to Mary Magdalene for her patience during the months that allowed the construction of this book. I made her relive painful memories, and it was, at times, not easy.

Thank you also to her children who faced their own memories with good will.

Mary Magdalene at 19 years old
© Marie-Madeleine Kabange Ngoie

This book was published on May 29, 2024,
in French on www.amazon.fr

Mary Magdalene is 33 years old
© Marie-Madeleine Kabange

ALAN

I first met Marie-Madeleine, without seeing her too much, in 2022, in a local cultural event, "Le Grand Bazar des Savoirs`.[1] We had three minutes to transmit skills to the audiences who wandered all weekend around the seventy "knowers" that we were gathered. I just remember a black woman, slender, very dignified, and very popular, supported by "go ahead, Mado!"

Almost a year later, in June 2023, I met her again in a volunteer intervention that I carried out for a local association, "Generation II Citizenship Integration."
I was helping the speakers of an eloquence competition to prepare their three-minute performance.
Twenty-two participants, from seven to ninety-four years old. She was a competitor in the senior category.
I remember noticing her phrasing in the "preaching" style, which was very effective, but whose tone could do her a disservice in front of a jury made up of local personalities.

I accepted the role of president-moderator of the jury.
She finished first in her category, with the congratulations of the jury.

I liked the atmosphere of the association and the values that accompanied all generations and nationalities in need of support. So, I continued to intervene punctually during the summer as a volunteer for support in expression, communication, and writing.
Over time, friendships were formed, but still not with Mary Magdalene. I met her regularly, but I had a panel of young people to take care of who were preparing a new eloquence competition for the end of August.

---

[1] Thank you from the bottom of my heart, Alexandra Lion, UNESCO Learning City Project Officer!

Along the way, the pressure of current events creating an annoying stress, the leaders of the association, to relax, resumed their usual chatter about each other.

"Madeleine, you are all alone. You are a widow." Can't find someone?

And someone said this:

"Are you looking for a white man?" Alain is alone, too...

By dint of chatting, a few days later, Anne-Sophie pushed one of the managers, Alima, to call me:

"Tell me, Alain: Madeleine, do you like her?" Because she likes you!

Surprised, caught cold, I stammered an answer that didn't really commit me, but that's how it all started...

Mary Magdalene is my exact opposite: the first thing to note is that she is black, and I am white. That's easy to see!

She is a little older than me by a few years, but she is not sure if the official date of her birth is the right one.

I am French, a "Parisian" intellectual, born in Paris and, like many, stateless in culture: of half-Savoyard, half-Norman origin.

I became a writer, but I have been working for years in the world of writing, communication, and networks, from the Minitel to the Internet. I grew up with analogue and digital photography, cinema, and media, and I grew old with the massive diffusion of new technologies, from the first Macs to AI on smartphones.

She is Congolese with an oral culture. She hasn't wanted to watch television since the Bataclan attacks in 2015. She doesn't go to the movies, she has trouble finding her way around social networks, and she has a poor command of her PC. But she has Africa in her heart and veins, and she learns quickly!

She speaks three languages, and she is learning English, in addition to being able to communicate with her grandchildren, while I only speak French.

She is a deep believer in an all-powerful, omnipotent God, while I am viscerally convinced that we are stardust and that I am resolutely anchored in a scientific and pragmatic approach.

She was an evangelical pastor, and I am a trainer on the Values of the Republic and Secularism.

She's afraid of everything, even superstition, while I don't fear much, and I manage my taboos.
She has faced illness, death and war and has faced them much more than I have ever had to.

Fortunately, we have common values, deeply rooted in us: an unwavering loyalty to each other, and a mutual trust that was established in just a few days after our first "serious" discussion about what we were looking for in a relationship.

We are both empaths, and we are extremely sensitive to each other's emotions, positive or negative.
We both cried while listening to "L'Affiche Rouge" by Léo Ferré during the pantheonization of Missak Manouchian and his wife.
The two of us tasted champagne to celebrate our first months of meeting.
Later, we shuddered, clenched our fists, and cried at the journey of "Malal", in Adama Diop's wonderful and fantastic multimedia show: "Fajar or the odyssey of the man who dreamed of being a poet".
We dreamed, danced, and hummed around Ibrahim Maalouf's trumpet.
We were both enthusiastic about the arrival of the Belém in Marseille and the passage of the Olympic Flame through our city.

We also share an unconditional love for our children and grandchildren and a fierce desire to survive, develop, help, learn, grow, and share knowledge and experiences.

I have three children and two grandchildren – for now – and she has ten grandchildren of her five children, all "children of the world":
I – Mylène, the eldest, is in Great Britain.
II – Marika is in the Congo.
III – Yves is in Great Britain.
IV – Melissa is in the United States.
V – Claudia, adopted at three months old, is in Congo.

It was obvious, an observation made from the first days: we were made for each other!
It was there, after some time, that she said to me, "Where have you been?" and I replied, "I was waiting for you!"

The more I know Mary Magdalene, the more I admire her career. It is a living symbol of resilience! She is not a heroine, but a woman who fights to survive, and who wins, step by step, day after day, with stubbornness... I learn, with her, to see the world differently than I have been able to before. She has an extraordinary strength, forged over the course of hardships. It forces me to argue on elements that I haven't thought about for a long time, to accept a point of view that is radically opposed to my own.

She believes that I have something "divine" in me... And that my "vision of the universe" is in line with hers... with the addition of that supreme being whom she wants to see in all things.
I open it up to science, from the living to the inert, from quantum infinity to the infinity of the universe and time.
In addition, she told me her story... That of an Africa full of bribes, traditions, witchcraft, and Kalashnikovs... An Africa that is looking for itself, with its children spread around the world who are fleeing death and violence, who wish to build their families in peace. A modern Africa where Custom,

nevertheless, remains alive and machismo: the place of women is not idyllic!

The unsaid is always more destructive than the "saying no!" So, her children, to her, I asked them to intervene, to tell their version of their story, in their own way... And their words, like their memory, have been freed. I'll let you discover their testimonies...

I wanted to share this life story with you in this book... You just won't have her Congolese accent, as I keep mine, Parisian, but everything is authentic... Respect!

Mary Magdalene (72 years old)
© 2024 Alain Avanthey

MÉLISSA – IV – USA

"Mom, your life can help others get by... So, write there! »

Mary Magdalene at 33 years old
© 2024 Marie-Madeleine Kabange

MAGDELENE

PART ONE: CONGO

I was born on December 12, 1951, in Congo, in Lubumbashi, and I have a twin daughter, Marie-Louise.
My mother gave me the name Mary Magdalene.
I still wonder why...

I had a godmother. On the day of my confirmation, I told her : "*Change my name, and that way, I keep your name.*" I wanted to take hers, Geneviève. She replied that "*No, no, you keep Mary Magdalene! Don't try to change!* ". That's when I understood that my first name was that of someone important.

For years, I thought I was the eldest.
In our country, twins, or twins, the one who comes out first is the eldest[2]: it is the one who stays in the womb who sent the other out. As I was the one who gave the "*kick-off,*" in fact, I came out second: it was therefore my older sister.

We were born in Congo, in the hospital of Lubumbashi, the capital of copper.
I had an older sister, Marie, who is now deceased, and later, I had another sister, Marie-Claire, and Jean-Pierre, a little brother. Jean-Pierre is still in Lubumbashi and Marie-Claire in Kinshasa.

My parents... Oh my, that's great...
There are many stories about my mother that I can't tell. It's a secret, until today. It is a story that does not leave me, but that no one will be able to make me break silent.

---

[2] Custom among the Balubakats (see below for more details).

I remember when I got married religiously, she was a little bored, my mother... With everything I know about her, she thought I was going to say it. I kept silent, but it bothered me a lot...

My father was a tall man, but my mother was like me, of average height, normal...

I don't know what happened in the house, but one day my mom left, and it was our father who kept us until we were married. We were six children, a boy and five sisters. Two of my sisters died today.

My dad worked as a cook for a Belgian. That's where we grew up, but mom was gone. We stayed with my father for a long time.

Mom remarried and had two children, or three, I think. The daughter I adopted is the daughter of one of my sisters on my mother's side.

I spent my childhood in Lubumbashi. It is a mining town: there are many mines, green malachite, and yellow copper.

I have just discovered the meaning of the stones in France. As I like to read, I look at what it means, and I have read that malachite helps fight pain. It is anti-inflammatory and antibacterial.

It is a mining town, with a lot of wealth and a lot of dust.

We lived in a house belonging to my father's employer, a white and Belgian man. He owned a large house, and he gave us a part of it already built on the plot.

He liked us very much.

I remember well. We went to his house, and he taught me to read, write, count, with his children.

I don't know if I was writing well at the time, but what I do know is that I was writing.

His children, they came to eat at our house. He got us used to his food, and to reading.

YVES – III – GREAT BRITAIN

> *It was a nice little house, a nice family, and it all dissolved, all of a sudden, like that... It hurts to think about it.*

My twin sister, I feel like she wasn't there. She had gone to my mother's side to my uncle's. That's where she stayed... I stayed with dad. What for? I don't know... I can say that I may be "*special*": my behavior was "*other*." She had her ambitions, and I had started spirituality a long time ago. It's not new.

THE CIVIL WAR

I remember, in Lubumbashi when I was with my father, there was a war[3]. I was twelve or thirteen years old[4], and Papa was still there.

I saw the men of the UN, Indonesians, Ethiopians... They were all there... I don't know what the war was... It was very, very, very, very serious! People were killed, and they were stabbed.

The Belgian gentleman had returned to Belgium.

We stayed in our house in the garden and the enclave to guard the Belgian's house.

MYLÈNE – I – GREAT BRITAIN

> *I went to Kinshasa in 2024, and you wouldn't recognize the city anymore. That has changed: the park has been landscaped, and we have built large apartments next to it. On the boulevard, there are holes, it's damaged.*
>
> *The house we lived in in La Gombé is still there, but it's a ruin: there's no one to maintain it, it's never been followed, and I don't know if we need to take steps to get this place back. It's destroyed. In any case, it should be done in a positive spirit, not looking at the past, but making it a family home, a house of joy. It would take a good lawyer to recover that. There are too many fights.*

---

[3] Congo gained independence in 1960. Between 1960 and 1965, the civil war caused more than 100,000 deaths. The intervention of the Soviets provoked the intervention of the UN, which sent "blue helmets". General Mobutu took power in a coup d'état in 1965.

[4] In fact, Mary Magdalene was nine years old in 1960. See below, on its age and the uncertainties associated with it.

One night, we were sleeping, I saw three soldiers who entered the house from behind. And now, they wanted to eliminate us, kill us all. I remember that there were three of them.

There, I took a blanket and hid underneath it because they were going to kill us!

Then, one of the soldiers asked to be left behind. And suddenly, they turned, climbed the perimeter wall, and left. I still have nightmares about it.

Later, it was Indians from the UN who gave us food. We would go to them, and they would give us water and cassava. It took a long time for things to calm down[5].

I GO TO SCHOOL

I was already praying at twelve years old. I attended the Sacré-Coeur school in Lubumbashi. They were sisters and a Catholic school. It began with primary school. There were no kindergartens as we know them today. You move forward, and it goes all the way to the humanities.

We were next to the presidential palace that was called "*Le Cinquantenaire*". I remember doing theatre there.

I finished my primary education, and then I went to secondary school. I couldn't get into university because my dad didn't have a lot of money for me to go on to higher education.

I remember very well.

I was thirteen or fourteen years old[6], and I was in the "*sixth year of secondary school*," as they called it at the Sacred Heart, and I often prayed. I would have liked to be a sister, or to be a doctor, or to have a midwife. Or simply to be like the "*Sister Help of Christians*[7]" whom I loved very much: she had studied medicine. A midwife...

But maybe I've become a wise woman.

---

[5] The UN Mission intervened from 14 July 1960 to 30 June 1964.

[6] Madeleine was probably about sixteen years old.

[7] Sister Help of Christians of Charity, a congregation founded in 1926, and missionaries in working-class and disadvantaged neighborhoods.

One day, while I was in the chapel, someone came to me and said, "*We want to get you engaged!* ". I see that he is bringing me a gentleman who comes from Zambia[8]. I looked at this gentleman: he was ugly! I apologize for saying it, but ugly! So, of course, I refused.

MÉLISSA – IV – USA

> *She was built by learning all this from the Bible. She learned to read and write from the Bible. She would spend hours and hours reading the Bible. She didn't go as far as she wanted to go in school, and she learned from the Bible. When I saw her at the time, it may not have meant anything to me, but today, I still get goosebumps: she also learned to speak well in the Bible. All the knowledge she has today comes from there.*

I loved people very much, so I often went to hospitals, alone, without anyone knowing, to see the sick: it was my passion to help them.

If I had a little money, I used it to buy bags of sugar, and I shared them. I decided on my own to go to the hospital to help and pray for the sick. I didn't treat them... Through prayer, perhaps.

I also asked the nurses what the patients needed. I saw wounds in the stomach, wounds in the limbs. So, I asked: "*How much does the bandage or the plaster cost?* or "*How much does the drug cost?"* ". And then, the doctor or nurse would tell me "It *must cost ten francs*[9]", and I would give them ten francs. On the bed, it was noted how much the patient had received and that he was therefore entitled to this or that bandage or medicine. Or even to eat for one or two days. I made several beds.

---

[8] Country bordering the south of the DRC.

[9] At the time, the currency was the "zaire", pegged to the CFA franc. The Congolese franc, also indexed to the CFA franc, was introduced in June 1998.

My birth language is Swahili[10]. We spoke French at the Sacred Heart School. I also speak Lingala[11], the language of Congo-Kinshasa. Three languages are a real richness, especially since Swahili is an international language. At school, we only spoke French: it was our father who spoke Swahili to us.

I remember doing theatre at school. I represented a lady, and I dressed very well, with a skirt.

At school, I was a scout with the uniform and the hat. We went into the forest: we learned to find our way when we were lost. I knew a lot of things, like that.

MARIKA – II – CONGO

> *In the Catholic Church, my mother was close to the priests. At each Mass, she was the one who prepared the altar, the books... She was a devout Catholic, and she did this service in addition to everything she did.*
>
> *We children were behind, and I was in the choir. We liked it.*
>
> *As I was in the choir, we were also in the scouts. We were in everything.*
>
> *This lasted until puberty...*
> *There, we had the chicotte[12].*

At the age of twelve, I already had emotions in prayer. I always wanted to help others, to give to others. I remember that there was a village with many sick people. I went with the sisters, and I washed their plates, I washed their house.

Often, from the age of thirteen to fifteen, I did it alone, and I came home late, I was keen to do it.

I could not imagine that this malachite, this beautiful stone, could be dangerous: I did not know it. They had wounds, they had diseases, but I worked, and I loved them.

---

[10] Language of Bantu origin. 150 million speakers in Africa.

[11] The Lingala language is also of Bantu origin. 20 to 30 million people speak it in the two Congos.

[12] A word of Portuguese origin designating a braid of hair or a whip. The Belgians used "*chicotte*" a lot in the context of colonization, to put the "workers" to work. The word is used here in the common sense of "*we could no longer stand still*".

I went alone, and no one sent me there.

> She dedicated her life to God: everything revolved around "what God said, what God did!" She is a spiritual woman who has dedicated her whole life to the Word of God, to the Lord. When I started to understand life, it took me in that direction. Nothing could be done without consulting the Word of God: it is this spirituality that has allowed her to live as she lives today. She is a "good woman" in the good sense of the expression, an example to follow. Me, today, everything I do, even if my head is elsewhere, I say: "Oh... Mom has never done that! So, me, at my age, why would I do that? ». She is my driving force, and I can recommend her to anyone, being sure not to disappoint. I know what she is, what she is passionate about, what she likes or dislikes.

When I met the father of my children in Lubumbashi, he also spoke Lingala.

I was already sixteen or seventeen years old, and he was two years older.

Later, he went to live in Kinshasa, and I followed him to his family. That's where I learned, Lingala.

FIRST JOB IN THE MIDDLE OF THE WAR

But let's go back a bit...

There really was a big war. And it took a long time, I remember. There was no food, there was no electricity, there was nothing. It was the Indians who gave us food.

Another day, later, when I was fourteen or fifteen years old, I found a job when things had come back to normal. I was an "executive secretary" in the Cofoco company. At fifteen, I was the executive secretary of a gentleman who taught me how to work. I had this grace.

From work, I bought myself a moped.

Blue: I remember, blue! A blue moped...

FIRST EMOTIONS

But I always went to school. One day, when I came back, that's where I saw the future father of my children.

I was wearing my blue-white uniform and a scarf, a small scarf. A gentleman approaches me, takes me by the neck, and says, "*You're the woman I want to marry!*"

His name was Yvon.
He was a handsome man.
He knew my twin sister, in Kinshasa, who worked with his own sister as a receptionist.

At the time, I replied: "*No!* and I left.

The days go by, the years go by, and I always think.
Another day, I had my moped, and I saw someone stop me, again. I stop, and we start talking. It was him again. "*Where do you live?* and everything!

He asked me where I lived and started coming to our house, "*to say hello.*"
But my dad didn't like boys coming to our house. He was very angry when he saw a man approaching his children. He protected me a lot.
One day, dad surprised him, and it became very complicated. But we were starting to be friends.

MARRIAGE!

His parents were also interested in me. They said, "*we're going to marry our son.*"
And for that, they tried to endow the girl.

We were married first customarily.
It's serious, Custom!
The parents of the future husband came to see my father to ask for his daughter's hand in marriage.
Before entering the house, they asked the neighbors.
Afterwards, they came back and gave my father three crates of beer. They said, "*This woman, it's not us who want her. We are not going to take her. It's our son who wants to marry her!* ".

It's called "*closing the fence,*[13]" and no one could take me. Touch me. They gave me the dowry in money, in my hand, and I accepted by passing it on to my father. Since my mother was not there, he also represented my mother's family.

As they have endowed me, he takes me, and we are married.

In Africa, when you are endowed, you enter the family of the husband. And I went to his family, still in Lubumbashi.

We went to the Commune, afterwards, to get married civilly.

A few months later, I became pregnant with Mylène, my eldest daughter. I was eighteen when she was born.

Well, eighteen years old... I remember that I was eighteen when I said yes to my husband, but in fact, on the official papers, I was twenty when my daughter was born. At the time, I didn't have much interest at my age. And in Africa, it's complicated... So, I don't know... Maybe my mother didn't give me or declare my correct date of birth.

My husband called me "*Mado,*" short for Madeleine, so many of my papers have that first name. And since I was a submissive woman, at the time, I didn't want to, I couldn't contradict him.

MY FIRST DAUGHTER.

For Mylène, the birth was complicated.

I had gone to the clinic next to our house. It was very early in the morning.

In the labour room, there was a woman who was bleeding a lot, a lot!

I was next to her. And this woman, so bleeding so much, asked the sister to leave her to take care of me. She felt that she was going to die.

I can still see her asking the sister that.

It was another sister who gave birth to me.

---

[13] "Kanga lopgo" in Lingala.

Mylène was born, and this woman left.
One birth, one death.

MYLÈNE – I – GREAT BRITAIN

> *There are not two, mamma!*
> *You breastfed me the first of your children, and I have always been your first baby #beaucoupdelove!*
> *You're special. The sound and effect of your voice on me are unique, especially in the morning when a good news phone call helps us worship the greatness of our Lord together!*
>
> *There are days when I say to myself: "Is this enough? What must I do? »... But you see, it will never be enough. Saying: "Mom!" is enough for me 100000000000000000000000000000000000000000000000 000000000000000000000000000000000000000000000000 00000000000000000000000000*

Mylène was very beautiful. Everyone came to admire her and to say something about her.

My husband's family welcomed me well at first.

There was jealousy among my sisters-in-law, and it became complicated. They hurt me a lot.

I didn't stay very long with them, because they went to Kinshasa, to one of the father's brothers.

My husband left with them, and they arranged, a little later, to pay for the ticket, to join them.

It was in Kinshasa that I learned to speak Lingala, and since then, I have never returned to Lubumbashi. My daughter Marika later went back to join her in-laws, but I never came back.

It was in Kinshasa that I learned that my father had died and buried. I couldn't go to his funeral.

I never thought about writing about my twin sister. We have two different destinies, even if we are physically similar...

> *Even we, when we were kids, we used to confuse the twins. They did their hair and dressed in the same way. They have practically the same smile. You meet the twin sister who has dressed in red, and then you meet Mom, also dressed in red, a colour she liked. When the two sisters were there, we often heard: "Where is she, Mom? Where is she? ».*
>
> *But we had found a trick: we had to make them laugh! Mom had beautiful teeth, but her twin had a golden tooth. Gold plated. It was this golden tooth that allowed us to differentiate them.*

It was when I grew up in the Congo that I realized that we were "*attached.*"

Every time something happened to me, it happened to her as well.

For example, if I had a toothache, she had a toothache as well and if I had a headache, she would have a headache as well.

I was almost into religion, and she worked as a receptionist at the airport for an airline in Congo.

She dreamed of travelling!

I was in the chapel all the time, praying. It was something else.

One day, a priest gave me his big rosary. I started using it, but very soon, I had weird dreams. I was scared, so I gave it back to him.

She was 17 years old, my twin, and in her work, she fell in love with a man who offered her a lot of money.

She agreed.

The gentleman took her, and they began to live together. But she was the third woman.

They had children together, six.

For me, it was something else: when I got married, it was "*normal*". The groom's parents came to us to give us the dowry, and later, we were married civilly in the commune. I was 18 years old.

And even later, when I had my four children myself, I got married in church. It was the bishop, whom I knew well, who married us.

He told me that I had to get married religiously because we were Christians. I am the only one in my family who got married in the Church.

I don't remember how old I was, but I already had my last daughter.

I never paid attention to my age.

MARIKA – II – CONGO

> *Her twin is not the same: if she meets you and doesn't know you, she makes you understand that she doesn't know you. She is tense.*
> *Mom, it's not the same: even if she doesn't know you, she greets you with joy.*
> *So, they played with it...*
> *Mom would listen to the person and then, at the end, say, "Oh yes... I would say it to Marie-Louise... ». And that's when the person realized that they hadn't talked to the right twin.*

When my religious marriage was announced, she cried, my twin, and she divorced her husband the same day.

Angry, he took me to court, saying that I was the cause of all this!

He had bought her a house, a car, and he didn't want to leave them to her. He found that the position of a third woman did not involve a religious marriage.

My marriage was spiritual: we were two different people, and she felt a little guilty.

Since then, we've had a good relationship, but she still wants to join me. She still wants us to be together. But I don't agree!

In Congo, I opened a hairdressing salon, the "*Salon Marika*," with an aesthetic part, and she also did the same thing because I had done it.

I had hairdressers working at my house and she took them from me. It made me angry: everything I do, she does! Everything I want to do; she wants to do. But I still love her.

MARIKA – II – CONGO

> *I never understood why, but when she had the idea of creating her hair salon, she gave it my name. Why not "Salon Mylène", or "Salon Meli", but why "Salon Marika"? I never asked him the question because very quickly, the "Salon Marika" took off. She took beauty courses; she did the hair of the clients herself and she also learned to do manicures and pedicures.*
>
> *And we, the children, have also learned this through her. We welcomed the customers who came, and we did their hair too. But they were willing to let it happen only if she was there.*

I did a pastoral ministry, and she got into it too.

It was strong, strong, strong... Every time I did something, she compared me, on my way of being and doing. I don't know if she was criticizing me, but...

MYLÈNE – I – GREAT BRITAIN

> *I spoke with your twin sister in 2024. She thought that your behavior was wrong, not correct. So, I reminded him that I had left thirty years ago. "I had just come back to bury dad. And then I left, and mom left, away from you."*
>
> *I left Kinshasa, I was twenty-two years old. I am fifty-two today. It's a lifetime! Mom has been gone for a lifetime, too.*
>
> *She told me about events between you and Dad, but it left me cold. I said, "Oh, have you been through that?" She said "yes". She has her own vision, images of "how you were treated by daddy," and she has her own wounds. And it's all because we love you! She tries to protect you because she thinks you're still hurt. I reassured her because I think you're much better. I asked her to pass on the message because, to this day, there are still people who ask themselves the question of how you managed to survive.*
>
> *Everyone has their own vision of things, even Mireille, a cousin I met in Lubumbashi who asked me how you are doing.*

> *And she added: "Mama Mado has experienced impossible things!" And I hadn't seen her for thirty-five years! I said to him, "And you accepted that? Was it too much, though? »*

MÉLISSA – IV – USA

> *One morning, mom comes to my room and plays me a radio cassette where her twin and one of her daughters criticize mom and us, mommy's children... It was shocking! They didn't know that he had a cassette that was spinning... They said rude things. Then they laughed...*
>
> *Mom reacted by saying, "Don't say anything, it's your aunt, it's my sister! I forgive him... »*
>
> *I was angry, but what to do: I had to stifle all my frustrations again... The relationship between mom and her twin has always been weird.*

When I won an eloquence competition, later, in France, and in 2023, I sent him the videos that were taken then.

She asked her children to check if it was true: she went to the wrong mailbox, and I received the message she had sent to her son.

I asked her why she was asking that question, but she just laughed back...

When we left Congo for Belgium, on holiday, with my husband and with her, she wanted the three of us to be together all the time. For her, it was "*we are united, we are united! »*

I remember too well what she did to me when I took her to Belgium.

In Congo, I had a lot of acquaintances with the Belgian ambassador, and his wife used to come to my beauty salon. So, every time I applied for a visa, it was easier. So, I ordered a visa for my twin girl. I paid for it, and everything... We left together with my husband, but when we came back, she didn't want to go back! When you apply for a visa, there are days that you must respect. You must keep your word!

She stayed for another three months, and then she came back, but it hurt me.

She always tells me, "*I don't see you, but we have to see each other!* " But I don't think the same thing.

When she wants to become a pastor, in turn, I don't think the same thing as her, I understand something different from her.
For example, today, I don't accept that someone comes and "*prophesies*" that a "*God told me that...*" I cut him off and told him that "*God is speaking to me too!* »
But she often says, "*God is speaking to me!* ".
When we talk on the phone, she often says, "*God is show-ing me this...*" ". She even told me one day that she had seen my photo in Heaven! But I'm always here to talk about it.

It doesn't hurt me, but it means that I'm not going to tell her everything. If I tell her everything I'm going through, it's going to hurt her. I, for example, am attached to Europeans to "*whites*" from Africa.

It's annoying this attachment between us. She imitates me in everything, and my children end up confusing us. Be-cause we look a lot alike, but also because she's trying to do the same thing I do.

But I don't want to. When I want to do something, I do it, not because someone told me to.

I don't know what really happened, but when my husband was in the hospital, she had a friend, and they lived together. When my husband died, she came to see me in the hospital with her friend. A few days later, he was also the one who died.
It was crazy, it was strong: all this because we are twins? I didn't like these coincidences...

It's so strong, this attachment that I don't dare to think of her for fear that she will call me. When she thinks of me to-day, she sends a message to know how I'm doing. I'm not really worried about that, but...

We are twins, we came out of the same pocket, but we are really very different. I understood that, but she didn't want to understand it. I don't even know if she's trying to figure something out... Why doesn't she talk to me? Why doesn't she call me?

I had a diary on which I wrote my thoughts and she said to me one day, " *Can I see it? You have a prophecy in it that I would like to see...* No way!

She wants to write a book, whereas I, since I've known a writer, I've been in it, completely. But I never told her about it... I've never thought of writing a book: my notebook has been for me for years.

I'm a widow now, but if I tell her I have a friend, now I know she's going to start imagining things.

She told me one day, "*You're not the same as me. Your husband, he's dead, so you can take a friend.*" But it's not up to her to tell me that: I know all this, and what I want!

My children are still in couples. They got married in church and honored their parents. All my four children and Claudia, my half-sister's daughter whom I adopted when her father died.

If my twin arrives tomorrow to see me, I won't be here: she's too complicated!

YVES – III – GREAT BRITAIN

> *A good memory... At home, we had a lot of animals and parrots. And every Sunday, we fed the parrots together with the parents. Mom gave me peanuts, and I had to give them to the birds. Dad was there, and so was Mum: they were joyful, warm moments. I liked to see them laugh and we could get together. Because of that, I took birds home, and the kids come to feed them with me. It makes us a family conversation, and it reminds me of my childhood when I was little.*

When I told my husband that I was pregnant with Mélissa, my fourth child, he got angry!

"We must take that away!" We must take that away!

He threatened me, and I, each time, cried: "*No! I don't take it off!* ".

It was a neighbor who came to console me.

When I gave birth, he didn't want to come and see her in the maternity ward. It's as if I had caused this pregnancy.

He had taken me to the hospital anyway, and when we saw the doctor, I told him: "*He is my husband!* insisting.

In anticipation of the birth, I had sold doughnuts and put the money in a bottle. It is this money that paid for motherhood. He didn't even want to buy the layettes.

A sister helped me, and Meli eventually came. She was an angel with a lot of hair. A very beautiful girl.

I asked my husband to give him a name, but he refused. So, I gave her my name, Kabange, Melissa Kabange! Melissa, because in front of us was a U.S. ambassador named Melissa W.

Since I was in a lot of trouble, someone told me to call her "*Melancholy*", but I held on!

As I was often told, "*My poor lady...* I replied, *"Everything is fine! Everything's fine!* ". And I had the firm assurance that God could not shame me.

This "*everything is fine!* I have kept it in the trials of the last few months... He has never left me.

When Meli was three months old, I started working again. Meli had become very beautiful, and my husband was starting to play with her.

My sister-in-law took advantage of my absence to repeat her lies. She wanted me to be driven out of my house.

I went through painful stories, but God always gave me strength. Our house, the one we rented from the state in Kinshasa, is a gift from God: I have always had a vision around this house. If this vision is standing, I will be standing.

The house
and the palm tree today
Photo taken in February 2024
© Madeleine
Kabange Ngoie.

There were some very happy moments in our marriage. Today, my children have understood, and they are looking to take care of me. They often call me: "*Mommy, mom!* And, at my age, it warms my heart.

MARIKA – II – CONGO

Every night, since I was little, every night it was prayer . We had to recite the "Hail Mary." We each had a rosary and a book, "The Book of Epistles." We were each in turn to read the passage of the day. Prayer was done early in the evening and in the morning. We grew up with this, "The Prayer Book," which means that today, when we speak, God is present in many of our words and actions. Mom and Dad wanted us not to turn away from that. They were there to protect us, it's true, but we had a God in whom to place our trust and faith.

YVES – III – GREAT BRITAIN

A few days ago, my son came to ask me to buy a guinea pig. I disagreed because they look too much like mice.
Finally, he won. I bought some, and last night when we were feeding them, I remembered that my first animal was a guinea pig. Mom had bought me one, then a second, which I fed with the parents.
And I do that today with my own children!

MÉLISSA – IV – USA

The story where Daddy didn't want me, you told me...
I cried for years. I even failed my year of school in second grade. I had lost control and I couldn't concentrate anymore at school. Before he died, Dad spoiled me a lot, but with that... I was in the dark. In me, it was black... I was looking at you, you were suffering... I decided to flee.

Mom, you hit me all the time! Of all your children, I think I was the wisest, of course! Of all the children you've had, I'm the most serious, the most loving, and the frankest (laughs). In fact, I reflect my mother (laughs). I am very friendly and very open. Everything I say has a meaning (laughs): it's me, my person! That's how I am! (laughs) I'm just like you! Even if I'm exaggerating a little...
Even when you were just hitting me!
At one point, I even wanted to die because it was too much...
But that's okay... I forgive you... You wanted to protect me... And of all your children, I think I'm the one who loves you the most (laughs).

You gave us, you made us dream, and for that, we will always be grateful to you. We really hovered until the moment when everything changed when everything went off like wind.
I prefer to keep those good times from before, which are engraved in my memory.

I'VE ALWAYS WORKED...

My husband had "*his occupations*," and his "*makeshift jobs*," but I have always worked. I'm not a materialist, but we had to eat.

MARIKA – II – CONGO

Mum cooked the foufou[14], but also the Mbika with good smoked fish and dried pumpkin seeds. The longest part is to shell the pumpkin seeds, then pound them to reduce them to powder[15]. It's delicious!

---

[14] Traditional dish made with cassava and other tubers.
[15] It is this powder that is called Mbika.

> *She also made good chicken with moussakas[16]. You cook the chicken, and in the meantime, you boil the palm nuts. Then, at the end, you pound them. By sifting, it gives you a natural oil that is very different from the palm oil used in cooking.*
>
> *She was preparing moussaka on the side.*
> *Then she would cut the chicken and fry it in palm oil, mixing it with spices. It was sublime, but today, I don't know how to do it...*

I sold cakes in a pastry shop, the "*Kilimanjaro*", run by a Belgian. I was a cashier, and the son of the President of the Republic came to buy me cakes. Later, he will come to my hair salon.

MYLÈNE – I – GREAT BRITAIN

> *I have a good memory of "Kilimanjaro," the pastry shop where my mother worked. It was a very strong period for her: she had a good job, saw people, had clients... She has people who love her, she is very beautiful, she earns her living, and she has her money. It is with this money that she created her hair salon. She was good. I remember that she arrived with trays of cakes of all models: pains au chocolat, croissants, pistachio croissants that I loved to eat... Frangipane cakes... Easter eggs, they were "as big as that"! There were also "club sandwiches"... And I told myself that there was something new in this couple.*

The bosses trusted me: when they went on holiday, they gave me responsibilities and I kept the whole shop. They had twin children. They loved me very much and helped me.

And even his wife loved me.

Since her husband was in the shop with me, people thought I was his wife. I was scared all the time, but since I don't like to hurt people, I put myself in his wife's shoes, and nothing ever happened.

---

[16] Moussaka is an eggplant-based dish, better known in Greece than in Congo.

YVES – III – GREAT BRITAIN

> *She also worked with Belgians who had a pastry shop. I liked it there, because, after school, that's where I went to spend my time eating ice cream that she served me.*
>
> *At the time, she had bought a Mercedes. I liked it because having a Mercedes was luxury, and it created joy. Mom had bought it, but the happiest was Dad.*

With my savings, I created my own hairdressing and beauty shop.

One of the President's children came to my living room to have braids made. I also did the manicure-pedicure for the second wife of the President of the Republic. They would pick me up at home, and I would go to her house. It was "*secret,*" and I worked discreetly. No one should have known, and they trusted me.

YVES – III – GREAT BRITAIN

> *Mom had a hairdressing salon, a sewing workshop... His hair salon was at home, and there were a lot of good smells coming out of there. There was also a massage parlor where men went to get massages. Good smells, in a good atmosphere: a positive energy that always animated it!*
>
> *It is with such positive energy that I am living my own house, today, to boost my children, if necessary. With all these memories, I can't give up.*
>
> *She had a lot of business. She stayed a lot with her employees: she really had a lot of them. Everyone liked to stay with her, to talk with her. It was a big family, but I felt a little abandoned: it was very active.*

MÉLISSA – IV – USA

> *I remember the time when my mother was working it was so good! I was so happy; I was growing up like a princess!*
>
> *One morning, I woke up, and everything that mom had bought for the comfort of the house, dad had destroyed it... Everything, everything! Jealousy crisis, I suppose... Mom bought everything back.*
>
> *Mom often cooked the kidneys in the evening, with just salt and spices, without sauce. It was so good! I sometimes do*

> *it here when I think of you, and my daughter Inès loves it when I show her things that her grandmother used to do.*
>
> *Once, mom made this dish. I would come home from school, and I was hungry. She had set the table very well. We had a glass table, round, very beautiful. Dad took the food and threw everything on the floor and broke the table. I was speechless...*
>
> *At the time, she had a hair salon called Marika, which was really doing very well. It was the first fair in our town. To complete, she also worked for Belgians in a pastry shop. In between, all the local authorities came to see her, and we lived well at that time.*
>
> *That's also how she travelled a lot: she was the one who paid for the tickets! She was the boss who took daddy!*

Later, someone came to me and offered to buy a yellow taxi. I had a little bit of economy, so I did. I finally got four, then six. And I wasn't the one who drove them.

A WOMAN ON A BUS…

One day, when I was going to pick up my daughter from school, I took the bus. There were two of us on the bus, and the rest of the passengers were men. I had taken the bus because it was getting late.

What I didn't know was that the other woman was pregnant and full-term. She started screaming. The baby was coming. The men began to shout at the driver to stop. There, we carried the woman under a tree.

The men said, "*There is only one woman here. It's you, so you're the one who must take care of her!* ". I had never given birth to anyone, but I could see that she had to give birth.

While the bus was leaving, with the men, I took a loincloth and surrounded the woman with very light protection.

She was starting to give birth, so I approached, greeted the child with my right hand, and rotated it so that it came out more easily.

I had braids, and thread of hair: I took a thread, and I measured a centimeter with my finger, from the baby's body, and I tied the umbilical very tightly.

I put the baby in the loincloth, and I pressed on the mother's belly to bring out the placenta.

The baby started crying.

Someone had called the doctor, and an ambulance arrived. I continued my way to pick up my daughter. I don't know what happened to them.

MÉLISSA – IV – USA

> *In fact, Mom thought I was doing stupid things. I had a lot of friends. And friends. There were a lot of people coming up to me, and mom was listening behind the doors!*
>
> *I was seventeen years old, and she had a very protective spirit: she chased people who were too clingy. It was natural for her! She fought for what she wanted. She fought for her family, and she protected her children.*
> *I thank her because she really fought for us to be what we are today. She is a strong woman, a loyal woman.*

WOMEN AND CHILDBIRTH…

It doesn't always happen so easily.

I had a servant – that's what they were called, at the time – who worked at my house and whose wife was already ten months pregnant. Wherever she went to see a doctor, and to give birth, she was refused. One morning, he came calling me:

"Madame! Madam!

"What is the matter?"

"My wife is in pain. she must give birth, and she is refused everywhere!"

"What do you mean, she's refused everywhere?" I'm going to take him to the Red Cross Hospital.

I take my car, and I take them both.

But he comes back to see me later that day:

"My wife is not giving birth..."

I get back in my car, and we both go back to the hospital. There, there was a sentry who didn't want to let us pass.

"I'm going to pray for the woman who doesn't want to give birth, and her husband, Dieudonné, is here!"

"What church do you pray to?"

— To the Church "*x*"
"Ah! That Church? With all that we hear as a reputation!
He let me in.
Before arriving in the room, the doctor intercepted me: it was not during the visiting hours.
"What are you doing here?!"
"I have come to pray for the wife of my servant who is accompanying me because she is not giving birth."
"What are you going to do more than us?"
"I?" I come to pray!
"Go! Come in!
When I came back, this woman came directly to see me. She was completely naked, with her big belly, and she knelt crying.
"Mama, pray for me!" Mama!
I picked it up, I supported it, and I said:
"You have to give birth now!" This child must be released now!
She went back to her bed and started screaming she was giving birth. The nurse finally arrived, and I helped them. She was so happy that she asked me to give the baby a name: I named him Jonathan.
Other women were having trouble giving birth, so I went to see them, another one, and another. And yet another. And the babies were born one after the other. A woman didn't want to see me and was turning towards the wall, and I think she died a little later.

A few months later, nine or ten months, I think, Jonathan fell ill: he was dying. Dieudonné calls me on the phone around midnight:
"Madame, Madame, Jonathan is dying!"
"Pass him to me, with his mother!"
And from a distance, it was too far away and too urgent for me to come and see them, I told Dieudonné to touch their hand, and I spoke to the baby and his mother:
"Jonathan, you mustn't die!" Why is that?
I began to pray from a distance, and I said to the woman:
"Touch him!"

And Jonathan woke up and got well.
He is still alive today.

Later, I met the manager of a travel agency. As I had contacts with Europeans, we worked together. She even became my son's godmother.

With the civil war, the Belgians returned to Belgium. They paid for my trip, too, and I went to see them. They entrusted me with a mission, that of taking care of their house in Congo and preserving it. I asked my husband to take care of that.

And then we got into trouble: the house attracted a lot of covetousness, and the government of the time tried to take it from us.

It is still inhabited today.

In Congo, there was a man who worked in an airline who had become attached to me. I was working in the pastry shop at the time, and every time the steward came, he wanted to take me away. He insisted that he would take me and my three children – at the time – and take care of them.

And since I was faithful to my husband, I refused. I told him, "*No, I'm married!* ".

I knew that if I left, my children would be destroyed. I put up with everything so that they could finish their studies.

When I arrived in France, it was the same thing: people came to me, but they were 40 or 50 years old. What would I have done with a man of forty, I, who was more than sixty? That's the age of my eldest son...

A lady once told me, "*Mado doesn't speak French well...*" *She speaks Lingala or especially Swahili!* because I came from Lubumbashi. So, whenever I could, I drank beer so as not to be ashamed.

I remember one weekday when I had to go to church, I bought a beer from neighbors, a "*skol*", very cold.

And the bottle broke in my hand. My right hand: I still have a big scar from it.

Since then, I have given up on the idea of drinking the beer.

CARDINALS AND CLAM FROGS...

Many people came to my house, such as the cardinal of Kinshasa or the priest.

They were the ones who asked me to get married in church because I was a Christian.

The cardinal, I had invited him the first time for Mylène's confirmation: "*Cardinal, I'm making appetizers for my daughter's birthday. Do you want to come by?* ".

I lived very close to the church, and he came in a cardinal's full uniform, in red, with the bishop, in purple, and the priest of the church, dressed normally.

It was the first time, for me, and the event, in the neighborhood. And it was a party at home, with the Belgian couple and my husband's family.

It was grace! I had planned wine, appetizers, pastries... Everyone was happy.

In church, I even gave communion.

During the service, I went to the sacristy in my white outfit. I open the box, I bow, I take the chalice with the hosts. Then I go up to the altar, I bow, I give the chalice to the priest who officiates, and I stand on my side. I remember well...

But when they knew that I had begun to follow the teachings of my evangelical church, the hostility grew.

I wanted to change something to understand.

YVES – III – GREAT BRITAIN

> *In the neighborhood, we were always in demand. She also worked with the Red Cross. On Sundays, she gave communion*

> *to the Catholic Church with the priests. She was the one who gave me my first communion and trained me in catechism.*
>
> *I don't know how it went from the Catholic Church to the Evangelical Church. I don't know what happened. Maybe she really wanted to take the microphone and speak, and in the Catholic Church, that wasn't possible.*

MÉLISSA – IV – USA

> *At that time, she also taught catechism classes in the Catholic Church. I remember one morning... There was a family ceremony and she had dressed very well... She was very beautiful in a white floral ensemble, soft green, made up, well-coiffed. She had a nice waist, thin, and she knew how to adapt her clothes to her figure. Her skirt was long, slit at the back. She had made cocktail rolls for the party. She had taught me how to do them too.*
> *Dad had to drop her off in the car. They leave, but five minutes later, they are back. She had a red eye: "Daddy slapped me!" I ask her why, but she replies: "Oh, I don't know!" She changed, did her makeup, and left like that.*
>
> *My dad gave me everything. At the time, I was going to university. I had my car – the blue Mercedes that my mother had bought, of course – and he had given it to me when all my elders left.*
> *I had a bank account that I had opened because every month I had my pocket money worth 100 dollars. That was a lot at the time!*
>
> *I have good memories of my father: he was very present in my life. I sometimes feel, until today, an emptiness in me. He wanted me to be well and independent. He didn't want me to depend on a man. I grew up like a princess.*

I was good in the Catholic Church. My relationship and my marriage were good. I had four children, and we lived in the Western way, a bit in luxury.

We even went on holiday to Muanda[17] by private helicopter.

---

[17] Or Moanda, a seaside resort by the ocean.

The beach was beautiful, and we were both good.

We rented a small boat, but there I learned what seasickness was. I read about it in the Tintin books, but this time, I lived it! Dizziness, nausea, vomiting: I had it all! We had gone to the point where David Livingstone[18] planted the English flag on the continent. But I was very sick...

And all this has brought jealousy again.

As I didn't want to have any more children, or I couldn't anymore, my in-laws pressured my husband to take a new wife who would be able to give birth.

MYLÈNE – 1 – GREAT BRITAIN

> *In fact, everything that Mom built that was positive was, in one way or another, destroyed later. It had to be broken, somewhere. It started well, and one fine day, dad broke everything!*
>
> *And Mom would start from scratch, as if she had never built.*
>
> *My father broke everything that my mother did: the good life at home, it was her! Travelling abroad, that was her! Our studies were her!*

One day, my husband started dating a very young girl, and it disrupted my life. With the help of his family, he took this young girl to her childhood village, and there I was lost. He installed it in a neighborhood not far from us. He took all her belongings and moved in with her.

I didn't believe this could happen to me, and I was looking for answers to my questions. I was screaming, crying, and praying because I loved my husband very much. I could not imagine that he was going to cheat on me. The Catholic Church did not answer my questions.

My husband distanced himself, and he left my house. That's when everything changed.

---

[18] Scottish doctor, missionary and explorer (1813-1873), famous hero of the Victorian era, who fought against slavery, but also for the development of trade with England and the evangelization of Africa.

I prayed and took up the Bible to find answers.

The world of women I worked with openly mocked me. And I almost didn't feel "*clean*." I was suffering a lot, morally.

I wanted "*this thing*" to be able to leave.

I prayed for help to get my husband and my couple back.

MÉLISSA – IV – USA

> *Dad's jealousy attacks began from mom's successes.*
> *At the time, Dad wasn't working.*
> *One day, he went to marry a 19- or 20-year-old woman in Mbujimayi[19].*
> *I remember seeing Mom lying on the floor on the floor for three days and three nights without eating or drinking, crying, and praying for the overwhelming disappointment of her husband.*
> *It was the "Fast of Esther[20]"... But I understood that fifteen years later.*
> *The girl is no longer there: she had gone mad and then died.*

One day, I was listening to the radio, and I heard the Pastor, the Bishop of the church, the Visionary, preaching.

I got in my car and went to his church.

It was full, and I couldn't get in: I stayed at the edge at the door.

I don't know why, but it was as if a light was shining on me, and the pastor was looking me straight in the eye. He walked over to me and began to prophesy to me.

I was attracted to it, and I started going there: it made me feel good. I asked myself questions: "*Is this really my place?*"

People were coming to me, and the Church Visionary was interested in me. I like to put myself in front of it, to listen better, but I don't like to put myself forward.

Later, I came with my children, but they didn't like it. They left, and I was left alone.

---

[19] City of DRC – Capital of Kasai Oriental.

[20] Esther 4 verse 26 – "*If I must perish, I will perish! »*

I began to take an interest in the life of the Church, and I made donations.

This became known, and the Catholic Church was warned: "*Magdalene has gone to an evangelical church!* ".

It's a bit like my life: I attract people without doing anything, and that still ends up causing terrible jealousies. I often find myself very alone, so I have learned to love nature. I went to the river, watching the boats go by. Where I would go to a park, and sit under a tree, to meditate and pray.

MÉLISSA – IV – USA

> *Many people looked at her, everyone talked about her: she was too beautiful, and she dressed... Oh my God! Me, it impressed me, to the point of falling to the ground.*

DEACONESS

One day, I was told, "*You are a deaconess.*[21]"

At first, I refused, and then I looked up in the dictionary what a "*deaconess*" was.

I saw that it was like a deacon, a servant, a boy in the House of the Lord. You look at what's damaged, like a chair, or if there's any mess in the room. That's how I saw the translation of deacon: " to *help in church.*" So, I helped: I even cleaned the toilets of the church...

It was a large church. I had a blue uniform, and there were about ten of us mother-deaconess. Every Sunday, we were dressed like this.

I was in my thirties. Between thirty and thirty-five years old, I think. I already had all my children.

CHURCH ELDER

After a year, or two years, one day that the Pastor, or the Visionary of the Church, was preaching, he approached me. I always stood in front of it, in the front row, to understand

---

[21] A woman who exercises a "women-only" ministry in some Protestant churches.

well. He comes there, next to me, and he begins to prophesy: "*God says to me... God tells me...* ". And he continues: "*God tells me, from this day on, you are an Elder, and I am going to ordain you and notify you as an Elder of the Church.*"

I was flabbergasted: the Elders can replace the Pastor when he is not there. So, I refused, again.

I stayed at home: it scared me! What was all that? I didn't like it, but in my dreams, I felt that it was a vocation. I loved being in church, I loved being with the sisters, and I loved helping others.

My life was hard, but I gave my clothes to those who didn't have any. And I gave without regret. I observed, and I gave, without my husband knowing.

I help easily, I give easily, I may not have, but I give to the other. In church, I gave a lot without my husband knowing. I even gave a large piece of land that I had bought in a beautiful neighborhood, to this Visionary of the Church: I gave him the papers, and my husband did not know it. I gave without looking. I also bought him carpets for his office.

I bought a lot of things without control.

That's how I am... That's how I am...

So, within myself, I ended up accepting what he proposed to me to do as an Elder of the Church.

I was asked to start talking to the people.

I was talking about how I felt inside, and it was good for the people.

There were a lot of people to come and listen to me.

As an elder in my evangelical church, I had to learn the Bible so that I could preach myself. I still have this Bible. It is full of my annotations, my scriptures: when you read the Bible, it takes you from verse to verse.

The day I got up to preach was a day of the week... Oh, Mom! The Pastor, the Archbishop, was standing there and watching me...

How should I speak?

I went for it, and from the first time, there were people crying, crying... And others who fell. In the end, they came to touch me. I didn't understand everything that was going on. I had done nothing.

The Pastor came to congratulate me: "*You have spoken well!* ".

That was a long time ago... When I was preaching, at the time, I mixed everything: French, Lingala, Swahili. I didn't know how to control speech and what I was saying.

When I was moderating[22], it was complicated...

To myself, I told myself that I had to learn, to go to school. So, I went to theology classes to figure out what I should do, how I should preach, and what. And also, to understand the Bible: I didn't really understand it.

I had many visions, and I would go to the pastor and ask him what it meant. But he didn't want to interpret them.

POISONOUS JEALOUSY...

Today, with hindsight, I say that in the Church, we did much more harm than good. Not everyone agrees. There are jealousies: this is what kills us, Christians, perhaps... I don't like to judge, but it's an observation I make.

I did it with love because I loved doing it: I began to feel my calling within me.

Until my husband became seriously ill.

Really very sick.

He had gone somewhere, to drink at a party, on a Saturday. I stayed at home. The next day, he started to have small pimples on his body, which turned into burns. It was horrible.

I went with him to the hospital. I was not afraid: I felt a voice resounding in my ear and singing to me, "*I am here! I am here!* ". And he gave me strength! A strength that I have never understood until this day. And every time the doctor came to touch his body, I would tell my husband that he would soon be healed, and I would chase the doctor away with a gesture:

---

[22] Period before the actual service, allowing the faithful to be prepared – to "warm" up.

"No! Exit! Don't touch him!

"*In My Name, I have given you Power!* and I knew I could help him heal by laying hands on him. I prayed and spoke words of healing to myself.

I had become stubborn, and no one could get close to him. I only gave him water to drink.

I didn't eat either. I was weakening, but I had the strength to stay by his side.

And I soon saw the result.

In my head, everything was mixed up a bit: it was complicated. When I said "*Jesus,*" I was obviously annoying people. So, when in doubt, I didn't want anyone to approach us.

When the family came to see us, there was a sense of unease: our spiritualities were different. I believe in my passion, but they...

Another day when my husband was sick, with a goitre, the family was shouting everywhere that he had to be operated on. I fought, in the name of Jesus: "*No, we won't operate on it!* ". And I did well!

Another day when I was bedridden, with a bad headache, they came to see me. I had the impression that something was on their minds. I had the bad impression that they didn't think anything good of me. So, I prayed, I prayed.

I was given medication, but it didn't work. So, I pray again, I believe in my God, and I'm healed.

Life is a struggle... God is powerful.

MYLÈNE – I – GREAT BRITAIN

During my time in the hospital, Mum would call me every day in London to give us news.

Alone, without strength, I had to take three days of a dry diet, without eating or drinking, with my eldest daughter Mychris, to pray for her recovery. Mom doesn't know that I struggled in prayer for nights for them. I had gathered a group, in secret, for collective prayers on his behalf. It was a very clear period: death was lurking. I remember it like it was yesterday!

> *At the end of this long tunnel, I was told that he was moving...*

Poisoned, then, my husband recovered! Every day, there were doctors who met to try to understand what he had and why he was cured. They finally came to an agreement and, like me, said that he had been poisoned!

When this became known, the hospital filled up with people who came to see my husband and pray with me.

MÉLISSA – IV – USA

> *I was 23-24 years old when my father was hospitalized at "Mama Yémo[23]" for "very deep burns."*
> *He went a month without moving. The doctors fed him through a tube, and he relieved himself on the spot. It was painful to see dad sick, and mom suffered for her husband. No one had access to the room, only the nurse.*
>
> *After my university classes, I would go home to see dad with my brother Yves, who was driving.*
> *But since we didn't have access to the room, we could only say hello through a small window that connected the room and the outside.*
>
> *When I arrived one evening, I heard my mother singing: "He's here, he's here, he's here..." ».*
> *I didn't understand anything. She had a desperate, tired, dejected face... As a child, I didn't understand anything. The only question that came to me was: "But how does she do it?" Unanswered! Listening to her sing, I thought to myself that, probably, she is talking about her Jesus...*
>
> *After a month, Dad was able to go home and had to undergo rehabilitation on everything... And I could hear mom singing, "he's here, he's here, he's here!" I still didn't understand and still assumed that she was talking about God.*

And despite all that, other people were talking about me in a mean way. That it was I who had hurt him! Men can be very mean in their words!

---

[23] Kinshasa General Hospital.

But because I had this strength in me, many came to my side to support me. And a week later, we came home.

After a month, the Church Visionary told me that I should baptize my husband.

I still have photos from that day in Kinshasa. I was there, but it was an elder who baptized him by immersion in the Congo River. It was also on that day that my daughter Melissa also had the immersion.

Melissa... At the age of three, almost died under the wheels of a car. She had decided to cross the street, and we went to get her under the hood, with just a damaged finger.

MÉLISSA – IV – USA

> *I remember this accident: I don't think I was three years old at the time, but nine or ten years old. And it was my nose and my face that were damaged!*

The pastor, at the same time, ordained my husband as an elder of the Church. We were then a "*Couple of Elders*," and he accompanied me to the church where I began to preach. I was replacing other pastors more and more.

When I was on the pulpit, preaching, my husband often motioned for me to go faster, that we had to leave.
When we preach, people come to the pastor to lay his hands on them, to bless them.
He also came, and several times he said to me, "*Ouch! You're hitting me!* ".
I was, all the time, embarrassed between shame and laughter.
He was serious: he is a man and he wanted to command me.

MÉLISSA – IV – USA

> *I remember when Dad was consecrated. Elder: Mom was happy, but I thought it was weird, and I told Mom.*

> *On Sunday mornings, Dad would change a large bill into small bills and distribute them to everyone, even Mom. It was to make a good impression and show the faithful that the children of the old Mado gave all the offerings...*
>
> *The small bills didn't even represent a dollar...*
> *Mom would say, "shhh, Melissa, take, don't say anything and give! It's your dad: it doesn't matter. »*
> *I was confused...*

PALM OIL AND SAKA SAKA

My husband planted two palm trees in the garden. Two oil palms. With the nuts, we made palm oil.

I cooked, and every day, we used it to make saka saka[24]. My husband insisted that we add the kernel of the palm tree, and I have eaten this all my life in Congo.

It's very fatty, of course, and it gives cholesterol. Since I learned this, I understood that I had to vary my diet and go on a diet.

MARIKA – II – CONGO

> *It was my dad who planted the palm tree in the garden. In fact, he planted three of them, one in the plot and two at the entrance, and they still exist today. I saw them again not long ago, and it was strong...*

A NEW CIVIL WAR

At one point, it was the end of Joseph-Désiré Mobutu before Laurent Désiré Kabila took power[25]. A troubled, dangerous, awful period. There were movements of revolt of resistance. We feared for our lives several times.

There were often curfews. One evening, while I was working at the pastry shop as a cashier, my husband came to pick

---

[24] Congolese national dish made with green leaf cassava ("*pondu*"), but also flour ("*foufou*") in couscous ("*attiéké*") and served with chikuangue ("*kuanga*" in Lingala – cassava bread).
[25] May 1997 – Mary Magdalene is 45 years old.

me up in his car. It was between six and five o'clock, and night was falling. We didn't know what was going on, but there was a strange atmosphere in the city. It was very quiet. In the neighborhood, there was no one in the streets. We arrived, put the car in the garage, and went out to walk around the house.

"Boya awa! Bangou! "Come here!" Quickly!

The order burst forth in Lingala with a wicked tone.

They were soldiers in camouflage uniforms, with foliage on their helmets and berets, almost invisible, and armed with small machine guns.

There were only two of us with my husband, and we were shaking in all our limbs.

Still in Lingala, and very curtly, they ask us:

"Where are you going?"

I managed to answer him:

"We live here next door.

"Where?"

"The house, there! Beside!

"Go! Hurry up! Quickly!

We were trembling, but we acted quickly. When I opened the gate, I found a lot of Mamas, on the ground, in the court-yard, Mamas, who usually sold bread at the offices in the area. As I was known, they had returned to our house to take refuge.

So, I sat on the floor with them, and I said:

"Let us pray together, God will protect us!"

And the shooting started at that moment. We were scared. Even the dogs didn't bark anymore.

This lasted all night. And when it stopped in the early morning, everyone went home.

Three of my children will end up going abroad.

We were in Kinshasa, and we lived in the commune of La Gombé, a residential area near the presidency.

Mobutu left, and two to three days later, Kabila arrived with his soldiers. There were "*Kadogos*[26]" in the streets of

---

[26] "Child soldiers" in Swahili. In 2007, they were estimated at more than 300,000, mercenaries enlisted in all the conflicts of the world.

Kinshasa. Between us, the "*Kadogos*", we called them "*the little ones*". There were many of them, armed to the teeth. They came from Brazzaville, on the other side of the river, and they were marching in possession of the country. We were a little obliged to cheer them...

There was fighting everywhere, bombing everywhere. The soldiers entered the houses, and there was looting and deaths. The sound of bombs made me sick. It was war.

At one point, Mobutu's son had an armoured vehicle, an armoured car, and he was shooting in all directions, and he machine-gunned the bank in front of our house, probably to take the money.

Another day, in the park of the house, there was a large, giant tree. One evening, from my window, I saw soldiers in the tree. Bembas[27], from the tree, waited for the enemy troops to pass.[28]

During the night, bullets began to whistle over the grounds of the property.

At that time, there were at least three "*presidential candidates*," each with their supporters agitating violently: Mobutu had fled, Kabila had been elected president, and Bemba had been defeated. The latter had created, with the help of Uganda, the MLC, the Movement for the Liberation of Congo: this entrepreneur had allied himself, then fought against the other two.

The Caisse d'Epargne, the bank across the street, was often the object of battle. Several times, we were asked to evacuate our houses, too close to the fighting.

We were crossing the street, but the bullets were whistling around us. A bullet passed very close to me, just as I was turning my head. The bullet passed and hit the soldier, a little further away...

---

[27] Supporters of Jean-Pierre Bemba.

[28] Mary Magdalene, still traumatized, mixes the dates of these two anecdotes: the first (Mobutu's son) dates from 1997, and the second (the Bembas), from 2006.

So after a while, we wouldn't move, and we would lock ourselves in the house.

It was really hot at that time. We suffered as much as we were afraid: it was too much.

AFTER THE SEIZURE OF POWER

I had my hair and beauty salon. As I spoke Swahili, I wasn't particularly bothered. I could talk with the "*Kadogos*".

I also did sew. Part of my hairdressing salon, on the first floor of my house, was a restaurant downstairs. The people from the bank next door came to eat at my house.

MYLÈNE – I – GREAT BRITAIN

> *I remember I was a child, and I always heard noises in the house. Noises, late at night.*
>
> *And if they weren't crying, they were beatings. I'm a child, I'm the eldest, I don't know what's going on, and I hear my mother screaming and crying.*
>
> *And not just any crying: you can hit someone, and they cry.*
> *But this was the crying of agony of someone who is tired of crying, but who has to cry because she is in pain.*

My husband was jealous to see all these cars lined up in the street. He was deceiving me. He was no longer quite living with me, but he was jealous and furious. He took money from me, hit me, took advantage of my connections, but he didn't like it.

MYLÈNE – I – GREAT BRITAIN

> *One day, I must have been five years old, there were louder noises, and I went down the stairs that led to the living room. Mom and Dad didn't know I was there and that I saw this above them.*
>
> *And the scene I saw wasn't good at all, at all.*
> *We had a big marble stone. I saw how Daddy broke Mom's finger on that stone. I also saw how he tried to cut his vein in his arm with a razor blade that night.*

> *I saw how tired she was, crying, how she was bleeding, almost naked, lying on the floor, and how he beat her.*
> *I saw him tear the skin off Mom's neck with his teeth.*
>
> *However, he picked her up and took her to the hospital.*
> *They put a bandage on her neck, and they put a splint on her finger, but she must not say anything.*
>
> *They didn't know that I had seen everything! And I grew up with these horrible images.*

YVES – III – GREAT BRITAIN

> *She was hit a lot, in her relationship, by dad, and that didn't do me any good. Once, one time too many, I stood up to tell Dad that this was not the way he should treat his wife. I remember that she had a lot of wounds and broken fingers. It wasn't a pretty sight. It also prompted me to leave the house.*
> *She was also fought a lot by her husband's family, and she didn't feel very loved by her sisters-in-law. She has been insulted a lot, and she deserves to be happy today.*
>
> *Now, with these bad memories, I try to keep a pleasant house without argument. I don't understand those who take a woman and mistreat her. When I think back to everything I saw in the house, I still feel affected. There's no point in getting married and talking badly to your wife.*
>
> *What consoles me is that the person who was insulted, to whom we spoke badly, this person lives.*
> *God gave him grace, and the other left before that.*

MYLÈNE – I – GREAT BRITAIN

> *At that time, Mom defended herself with prayer, but I know that there is more to these problems than prayer.*
>
> *I couldn't do anything: I was vulnerable, a little girl. I don't know what is going on, as we continue to receive family members. There are meetings, discussions, I understand that there are complaints, but I can't speak.*
>
> *My vulnerability has made my character. I was overwhelmed as a little girl, then as a young girl: I couldn't stand men! I came close to homosexuality because of that. I felt much safer with a woman. A man, for me, was this image of my father that accompanied me until I was twenty-five.*

> *Dad's family? I haven't seen one of Dad's family be close to Mom! Daddy's sisters and brother, they gave the impression that they were not happy to see mom and dad together. At one point, before dad's death, mom completely adopted silence... She didn't talk when they were there.*
>
> *One day, in front of me, one of my dad's sisters wanted to insult mom. I reacted by saying, "Stop! You don't talk like that to mom! She left Mom alone. It was so much of it, overwhelming, exhausting, overwhelming, troubling, frightening...*

There was Custom, and in its name, they killed! If I had agreed to leave, there would have been deaths. I didn't want to take away the secret of the house.

> *The weight of custom... In my dad's family, there were eleven brothers and sisters. He was the ninth. Before mom, there were nine women: the first, the second... She was one of the "young" sisters-in-law. And they made him see all the colors.*
> *She didn't let herself be done, but it was complicated. She was obliged to defend herself because who was going to do it in her place?*
> *We were the youngest children. In this family with very strong traditions, "talking" was already disrespectful to the elders. So, we had to put up with a lot of things.*

The children had to grow up and study. I couldn't transfer that pain to them. Then, whatever might happen, "*everything was fine!* »

> *In Kinshasa, life has nothing to do with fifteen years of your life here.*
> *I left thirty years ago. That's a lot. I have left you for thirty years. I wanted to continue my studies in Europe, and I was convinced that I would feel better "outside" outside the country. I also believed that if I left, I would be able to support the family more easily.*
> *We had just passed the Second Civil War. I felt that the good life we had was starting to fall apart. The shop where my mother worked, it wasn't going as it used to be. And I felt*

> *that as an eldest, I had to leave, to find myself and find a new lease of life.*

For me, what mattered was that my children could continue their studies, have their diplomas, and take care of themselves. They ended up finishing their universities, making beautiful marriages. That was the main thing for me.

MÉLISSA – IV – USA

> *As I grew up, I understood that she was looking for peace within herself because fear was part of her daily life.*
> *Fear of experiencing another humiliation, fear of a new betrayal, fear of experiencing a new aggression...*
> *The spirit of God gave her peace, so that's why she sang. I saw her cry while praying, but she had to keep coping: it was hard to see this without being able to do nothing.*

I had many activities. I had an association, Amagode, which took care of single mothers but also intervened in environmental problems. For example, we painted to beautify the neighbourhoods.

MARIKA – II – CONGO

> *One day, she woke up and, I don't know why, she told us, "I'm going to apply! To the municipality... I will be a candidate! ». And here she is launching into the electoral campaign.*
> *At first, we took it as a joke. But when it passed... Dad started to congratulate her, to encourage her, but we were all surprised... To say that she is a fighter and that she never gives up! When she decides, she pursues it to the end.*

When we needed contact, I was consulted. By dint of it, I became the "*head of the neighborhood*", the "*referent*", chosen by my neighbors. When there were funds available, I had to dispatch them. I had a lot of connections...

THE CREATION OF THE CPPs

And then he had the CPPs[29]...

---

[29] The "*Committees of Popular Power*" created in 1999 by LD Kabila to counter the traditional parties and "*monitor the Congolese people*", very

It was impossible to ignore them, so we had to know what they were doing. If you weren't from the CPP, we created problems for you. There was no opposition party. They were all banned.

YVES – III – GREAT BRITAIN

> *One day, she went for military training with the CPPs. The government was asking people to go to the army to train, and mom left. It's a memory that makes me laugh today.*
>
> *When she returned, the soldiers had put them in single file, like well-trained little soldiers. In the crowd, I was looking for mom, and I saw her walking like the others. It still makes me laugh.*

MÉLISSA – IV – USA

> *She gets up one morning, I don't know what happened to her, and says, "I'm going to Kibomango, to the soldiers, where they are trained to learn how to defend me and learn how to shoot a rifle."*
> *And it leaves us!*
>
> *I was sixteen or seventeen years old at the time, and I was a pretty ... Boiling... And it really didn't mean anything to me that she was leaving! Mylène was already gone. Marika was already married.*
>
> *Mom was away for two weeks and was trained like a soldier. And when she came back, she had a different mind. She was a completely different person, a fighter ready for anything!*
> *She wanted to deal with domestic abuse.*
> *And her life changed: she knew what she wanted, or she didn't want it anymore! She could finally say, "No!"*

CANDIDATE FOR DEPUTY?

At one point later, I applied to be a member of parliament, but I was "*screwed up*". I had projects and beautiful projects.

I know who "*screwed* me up. ": one of my relatives, whose name I will not mention, who gravitated in Kabila's

---

quickly became a tool of power. The "*excesses*" of this "*security force*" led to international investigations into human rights violations.

small circle, opposed my candidacy. What for? More jealousy, no doubt, but maybe more.

My best project takes me to the Minister of Agriculture. He receives me, approves my file, finances it. But I don't know where the money went: it never reached the association, on the ground.
I was very lucky, but also very naïve.

MYLÈNE – I – GREAT BRITAIN

> *I have often been told that my mother is "tough"... No, she is direct, and she has a pure heart. She evolved with a pure mind. Today, I continue to respect what she says.*
>
> *There are days when I am revolted, in my mind and in my heart: it is anger!*
>
> *A devastating anger! It is born because of what I have experienced and seen! You must heal completely to find peace.*

OF REGIONS, CUSTOMS, AND PEOPLES

Laurent Désiré Kabila was from the same region as me, and his son, because he had a twin, was called Joseph Kabila Kabange: Kabange, like me who is Muluba who speaks Swahili.
It is a tradition in our region of Katanga Muluba[30] to give the name "*Kabange*" to someone who has a twin[31].
My full name is Marie-Madeleine Kabange[32] Ngoie. Kabange because I have a twin, and Ngoie is the name of my dad.

He, JK Kabila Kabange, became President of the Republic in 2001 after the assassination of his father.

---

[30] It's not easy to explain... Muluba: part of the Luba people. Region of the Luba people (the "lost") – The Baluba-kats: the Luba of Katanga.
[31] Marie-Madeleine, who left second, inherited the name "*Kabange*", while her twin sister was nicknamed "*Kyungu*", the eldest.
[32] Pronounce "*Kaban-gué*" and "*ngoïe*".

The father of my children was from Congo-Kasai. My children therefore have Kasai origins, on the father's side, and Baluba-kat, on the mother's side.

MYLÈNE – I – GREAT BRITAIN

My dad had his mentality. He saw things his way: if you weren't for him, you became an enemy. He made you believe that mom "wasn't the right person" and that we all had to get on her side. But it was he who made everything difficult. There were moments of joy, of deep joy, but we went from joy to pain, and as joyful as it was, as painful as it was, it hurt.

As I grew up, I could see that this didn't change there were many scenes of bloodshed! And I understood over the years that mom couldn't stand it anymore: she started to defend herself. And the defence became a fight in the house. She had had enough and was reacting.

MÉLISSA – IV – USA

Before, it was difficult because she was a very beautiful woman, submissive, who accepted everything.

My father, out of excess of jealousy, thought that my mother was cheating on him. It pushed him to hurt her, not realizing that he was breaking up their marriage and shattering a life with a woman who loved him. It must also be said: mom loved him very much!
When she came back from her military training, it all went off in the wind! Even the mother-child relationship was different. We were dealing with a soldier, in front of us, at home. She had become twice as tough, really a different person.

MYLÈNE – I – GREAT BRITAIN

One of the scenes I still remember turned my life upside down... I was at my grandfather's house, and I saw my mother arrive with her whole face deformed, swollen, bleeding. Grandpa asks what is going on, horrified. She was crying and saying, "I can't take it anymore!" I don't know what he beat him with to make his face so damaged. He came back to get her, and she came back.

One day, my son Yves found himself cornered by the army. He was strong and tall, a giant, even then, and he drew attention to himself.

I was driving home from church. I wanted to get back very quickly, but instead of turning left, that day, I was turning right. It was there that I was stopped by some Shégués[33] from my neighborhood. They knew me, and I knew them, so I stopped to figure out what they wanted to tell me.
"Mama! Mama Amagode!

They knew my association Amagode and called me that. I stopped the car, and then I heard my son Yves screaming as he was being hit!
There were four soldiers from the presidential escort surrounding him and beating him.
I asked them why, in Swahili, and they explained that the kid had not stopped while the national anthem was playing. The kid didn't know that he had to freeze, then.
"Mamma!"

I kept my senses and chose to go apparently in the direction of the military:
"No! You have done wrong! You can't march during the national anthem!
And I slapped him!
When the soldiers saw that I was not "*happy*" with my son's behavior, they began to smile. And still in Swahili, they said to me:
"Go! Just give us some cigarettes, and we'll let your child go!" And next time, it won't be the same!
I had some money in my pocket and gave them "*for the cigarettes*". And they released him, and I took him home.

---

[33] Street children and teenagers – often abandoned by their parents, they organize themselves into gangs to beg and survive.

YVES – III – GREAT BRITAIN

The most striking memory that I keep in my heart is that my mother saved me from death.

As far as I can remember, I was seventeen or eighteen years old, and I was walking around my neighborhood.

The presidential motorcade passed by at that moment and apparently, when the presidential car passes, everyone must stop without moving their heads or arms.

I didn't know that I had to stop, and I kept walking. All the soldiers turned to me, and they beat me like a dog.

They were beating me up, and there was blood everywhere.

A policeman said, "We have to kill him!" and the chief said, "Shoot him now! Shoot it down! »

Mom was coming back from church, and all the people in the neighborhood said to her, "Your son, your son!" And she came.

I had lost consciousness, but she spoke with them. I don't know what she gave them, but they let her go, telling her, "Go home, and make her a white chicken," because I had escaped death.

In the evening, when I got home, I saw my parents: they were so dejected, their faces marked by the sight of their son with blood everywhere, their clothes torn, and above all filled with remorse for not having been able to defend me. I saw all this in their eyes.

It's a striking memory because that's why I'm in London today.

After being tortured like that, I told dad that "this was no longer a country for me."

It is this situation that forced me to leave Congo. Every time I think about it, I tell myself that if mom hadn't come by at that time...

Without it, I wouldn't have even tried to leave.

Another day, I go to my veranda, and I hear a whip cracking in the park. And I also hear shouting, *"Mom!"*

It was Yves, surrounded by Kadogos. He had wounds everywhere. They tried to scare him so that they could enlist him.

I spoke to them in Swahili, and they eventually left.
But that's also why I wanted him to leave Congo.

YVES – III – GREAT BRITAIN

> *When I was a child, I went to the gym and body building every day. I spent my youth in gyms.*
> *I started very young, for... protect mom...*
>
> *I was strong, tall, and strong for my age. As a result, in Congo, I was bothered every night on my way home and attacked at least three times by the military or militiamen who thought I was a rebel.*
>
> *She always organized my birthdays, and she took good care of me. I was always well dressed. Every night, she came to put me to bed and put me with ointment. I am very happy when I think of her, how she took care of me.*

FROM KINSHASA TO BRAZZAVILLE

I miss my pastoral ministry very much.

One day, the army entered the church, and they started beating everyone, just like that, without warning, without provocation.

I went to hide under a table and prayed.

They kidnapped women and old men. All this because the Pastor had angered a president. Complications between opponents, a story like that...

In fact, they wanted to arrest the Pastor! And for that, they kidnapped many of the faithful, wounding their legs, feet, fingers... It was crazy. They quickly released everyone except the Pastor who went to jail. There, he fell ill. It was strong.

Later, I was sent, as an Elder of the Church, to go and preach in Brazzaville. It was the first time I had gone to Brazzaville, crossing the river in a canoe, and I had been given a one-month mission. I made the trip alone. I was scared. It takes thirty to forty-five minutes, the crossing, and it was the first time for me.

Every month, we were to celebrate prayers on the theme: "*God will provide for the Mountain of the Lord*[34]." In the Bible, Abraham went up the mountain to sacrifice his son Isaac.

The prayer lasts seven days in a row. The pastor of the place was a young man. At that time, it was his church, and I was the one who had to replace him.
He welcomes me as an Elder and takes me to the Church downtown.

Finally, I arrive at four o'clock and he introduces me to the church. It was full.
He calls me "*Mom*," like all the Elders.
He said to me, "*Mama Mado, you are going to speak, and you are going to lead us to this Mountain of the Eternal God will provide.*" He had to go and preach elsewhere, and he gave me a prayer to let me accompany his people.
And finally, he leaves me there.

I stood up, took the microphone, and introduced myself.
I preached the story of Abraham, who was led to sacrifice his son. What faith he had!
Before arriving at the Mountain of the Lord, he told his servants, "*Stay there!* ". They stayed, and he continued with Isaac.
Isaac finally said to his father, "*Father, I see the knife, but where is the animal? »*
I spoke as if I had lived the story.

And then, at that moment, people went into a trance. They were shaking, they were crying, and I was crying too.
The church was mad when I wasn't done yet.
I spoke, and the mothers collapsed on the floor. Others sang or said, "*Mado, speak! Talks! Talks!* ".

---

[34] Genesis 22:14 – "The Mountain": symbolic image of the Temple and the encounter with God.

Years later, I still have chills: it was an atrocious stampede. I didn't feel well: I felt like I had been poisoned by evil prayers. And at the end of the week, I stayed sick for a long time.

There, people were rolling on the ground.
And there was a woman in a wheelchair. She couldn't walk. So, I came to this woman, and I said to her, "*In Jesus' Name, get up and walk!* ". And she got up and walked!

It wasn't me, but it spread everywhere until the Church Visionary came in and asked what was going on.

That's when I felt that there was a lot of jealousy in the air, and that in Brazzaville, they were going to kill me. Otherwise, I would have made a lot of progress in my ministry.

It was from this impression that I began to doubt, to give up everything: in the Church, we hurt each other far too much, and I was hurt far too much. Today, it's my children who continue, but I've let go.

After that episode, people came from all over to see me. They were crossing the river, too. They wanted to touch me.

Marie-Madeleine
(45 years old),
her husband Yvon,
and Melissa
© Marie-Madeleine
Kabange Ngoie

I don't know what was going on, but it happened several times with sick people. The last time was in France, with a colleague who, suddenly, fell, convulsed.

She regained consciousness as we called the fire brigade. And she started screaming, "*I'm going to die! I'm going to die!* ".

I walked up, took his hand, and spoke in his ear, "*You can't die like this...*" *It's going to pass!* ". I opened her bodice because it was very tight, and she started laughing. The crisis was over.

To come back to Kinshasa, there was a Bishop, a Bishop, a Pastor. The Bible always speaks of Servant, Pastor, and Shepherd, but he was called Bishop and no longer Archbishop. One day, he called me: "*Mama Mado, you have to go and replace a pastor who has gone to preach elsewhere. You're here, you're going to go and preach at the assembly, in the city Centre.*"

The "*downtown*" is Church *"x"*: a crowd of believers of at least five thousand people. So, I stood up and picked up the Bible, and I spoke.

When I preach, and I tell the Bible, I try to bring the episode to life, I visualize the places where it happened and how it happened. I put myself under the hat of the witness, who was there, and I tell the story, speaking normally. I don't really know how to explain it, but it pushes people to relive history. So, they went to the other side, to come and touch me.

A DEACONESS WAS LOOKING AT ME

It was at that moment that I saw the face of a deaconess looking at me: she was sweating jealousy. She was confused. She was a very beautiful woman, but the Visionary cared for me "*because I had something.*" So, I saw in that look what was going to happen or was supposed to happen.

In fact, in that period, I was not considered, I was not allowed to move forward. Finally, the Visionary sent me to Paris, with the mission of being the Pastor of Paris and developing a new church.

MY CHILDREN…

My children are all educated. My husband continued his occupations, but I worked to pay for our children's education. I took them on a journey, like my husband, when he was alive.

Customs are thus... After giving birth to Mylène, I was breastfeeding her. She was very pretty, a beautiful creature. And when I was three months old, without explanation, one of my sisters-in-law took it away from me for the month of her vacation. Later, at the age of twelve, they took him to his paternal grandfather's house. I didn't see her again until a long time later. A little before she left for London.

MYLÈNE – I – GREAT BRITAIN

I have no memories of having been to my aunt's house. My first childhood memory is a photo of my mother that I hold by the hand. I must have been between two and three years old[35]. This was at a time when the house was not fully built: there was no surrounding wall yet. Over the years, the house has changed, and walls have been raised. But this same house,

---

[35] 1974 or 1975 – Mary-Magdalene is 24 or 25 years old

> *today if you go to see it, there is nothing left, it is a ruin. Anyone who passes by is shocked. "Papa Yvon and Maman Mado lived here? What happened? ». Someone asked me if there was really anything I could do to get that back.*

My in-laws hurt me a lot.

So, this girl, Mylène, she, has been praying for a long time because she has been persecuted.

I still don't know which custom it corresponded to. Maybe something that escapes understanding.

I had faith and I still have faith.

MYLÈNE'S PROPHECY.

One day, while Mylène was in my hair salon, a giant African man entered, a little red-haired, a little light-hearted, and remained standing in the hallway.

"Hello?"

But he doesn't really answer. He turns to Mylène, and begins to prophesy her:

"You're not going to stay in this country forever." You are called to leave Africa to go to a foreign country. We have to do it now!

And he leaves!

He had only spoken to Mylène.

There was no money for a trip. I was the one who had the money, thanks to my hair salon, and since Mylène took it to heart, we started looking for the funds so that she could travel.

MYLÈNE – I – GREAT BRITAIN

> *My father was violent, and violence doesn't speak to me. I didn't experience dad's violence like my sisters and brother. I don't know how they really felt because I left them. But I experienced things in my early childhood that made it impossible for me to stay there. I had to leave, and in time, bring mom over.*

Mylène said to me:
"Mom, only you can do it!"

Women always keep a little money aside for a rainy day, so I took the money.

MÉLISSA – IV – USA

> *Men, sometimes, can depend on their wives...*
> *I don't know what happened in mom's companies, but she ended up at zero. Everything was turned upside down, like a breath.*
>
> *Her marriage had become very difficult.*
> *He's my daddy, and I don't want to say anything bad about him, but...*
>
> *We children, there was a moment when we decided to protect her, because it was too much. She was beaten, mistreated, insulted, and so on. Until he had a broken arm. The man pushed her to a point where she wanted to leave. But because of her children, she decided to stay, to protect us. She said all the time: "I stayed because of you!"*
> *The Bible and God also helped him to hold on: they were his only allies, and it gave him the strength to stay. Resisting all this made her the strong woman she has become today.*

We had family in South Africa: we went to the Embassy to get a visa.

By acquaintance, we were introduced to the embassy by the mother of a friend of Mylène's, Sandy. Sandy was the girlfriend of Yves, my son, and Sandy who became his future wife.

We hadn't told my husband because we were afraid that he would ruin this trip before it even began.

Mylène started to do the paperwork and got her passport.

She was 14 years old, so for the visa, it was something else! The father had to authorize the departure from the territory...

I don't know how it was done – God is good – but one day, the visa came out with the authorization without the father intervening.

Money still had to be found. Mylène has decided to go see her father:

"Dad, I got the visa, I have to go!"

He resisted, but three days before the start, he accepted.

Another curious point: I don't know who had told her that a child of Mado's was going to South Africa, but Christian's mother gave a letter to Mylène asking her to hand it to her son.

Christian, whom Mylène did not know, was to become her husband.

Last avatar: On the day of departure, there was no money for the ticket. No one had bothered about it.

I had a little bit of reserves left, and I paid for the ticket.

Mylène got on the plane, and she left.

I cried a lot, and I still cried.

MYLÈNE – I – GREAT BRITAIN

> *When I managed to talk about everything I had seen, I was already grown.*
>
> *But just before leaving, I confronted Dad.*
>
> *I was outside, he was talking to me, giving me advice. I was listening to him, and when he finished, I said, "You know, I've grown up! And I don't think you're telling me the truth! You always want to look the best, but in reality, it's not really that! I think you need to change! If mom stayed at home, somewhere I think you must change! ».*
>
> *He stopped talking and just went. "Ah... So, you're for your mother? ».*
>
> *I told her, "I'm neither for her nor for you! I am for my parents, and I am for peace! I am leaving, and I do not know how I am going to leave you!" »*

When I arrived in South Africa, my husband's family was there, waiting for him at the airport. But very quickly, she was made uncomfortable: they didn't accept it.

> *I was in South Africa. I kept hearing all kinds of stories. Who could possibly believe me? I don't know how mom managed to get out of it, how she could deal with this person who was beating her? And that's when I wrote to my dad.*
>
> *I wrote him a letter of six or seven pages, a long letter. And when he received it, he was not happy. I mentioned the scene I saw when I was five years old. And then, I was over twenty-five years old.*
> *I was told afterwards that dad had cursed me! It was Yves who told me that! He was also not happy! I had gone straight to the point: I wanted dad to stop it! I threatened him to ask for a family reunion, to come back to Kinshasa to solve the problem or to take my mother with me to go to Europe. I told him he was going to stay alone!*
>
> *He didn't like this letter and took it to the whole family talking about me in a mean way. He said bad things about my life. But thanks to this letter, even if the change was not one hundred percent, I heard that things were calming down between mom and dad. The gap was big, but Dad was starting to go to church, and he was a little different.*

To escape this situation, Mylène first decides to give the letter that has been entrusted to her to the person concerned.

It was there that they met for the first time.

Christian helped Mylène find a room so that she could be comfortable.

After a while, Christian sent a letter to his family to say, "*I want to marry Mylène!* ". Christian's mother, therefore, begins to look for the reputation of Mylène's family, as is customary. They did an investigation in the neighborhood.

And Mylène called me so that I could go and see who Christian was in South Africa.

"Mamma, you come!"

I went to South Africa, I met Christian, and everything went well.

MYLÈNE – I – GREAT BRITAIN

> *Dad could be adorable, and we had a good life in the house. And even if he loved you, suddenly, he could be subjected to demonic, satanic spirit that took power. Perhaps he was looking for deliverance. It was mom who was subjected to aggressive, abusive behavior.*
>
> *And then he would become "normal" again, for three or four weeks, she had to accept and start again. He broke everything in the house, and she bought everything. Until the next crisis.*
>
> *This "animal" spirit is not human. I learned that the Custom has been dealing with this since the great - and great-grandparents: the woman has no value.*
> *I understand my mother, who said, "if I change my life, it will be with a blank."*

But when I returned to Kinshasa, I had problems, strong problems with the family!
"Why you?" It was your husband who had to go!

MYLÈNE – I – GREAT BRITAIN

> *No one knows what you're doing and where you are. The people you knew have aged. You're not going to dream of seeing them. You're not going to like them. Some have aged a bit... They look like little old people, even if they are younger than you!*
>
> *What we thought you were going to become; they became the ones. They only know that you're doing very well.*
>
> *And they saw me: thirty years later, I know that I don't look my age compared to those who live in Congo. I'm "fresh" while they have old people's necks and old people's skins. I'm good, I'm fine, I'm talking about peace, love, life! I'm not in the past, so they don't build! I don't hold a grudge, and I said hello to all those who have hurt us! I smile at them: they see me passing while they are motionless! On site, I have a nice car, a nice house, I eat, I laugh, I'm fine! In the street, I am told "Pastor", and when I arrive in a house, it is "Ah! Mado's daughter! or "Ah, Mylène, the Apostle! ». The honors is there!*

In the meantime, the preparations for the wedding were progressing. Christian was a doctor. He had a good job and earned a good living, and he wanted to have an extraordinary marriage.

To marry Mylène, for example, he organized everything in a large hotel.

We had to prepare. We bought clothes...

But now politics gets involved: Christian's family was on the Mobutu side of the Congo, and we were on the Kabila side. In fact, her family fought Mylène, and I remained in prayer until the end. His mother didn't want to. His family didn't want to, but Christian stood his ground.

So, his family delegated people to testify about the wedding, and on my side, I had people who came to my hairdressing salon and told me, "We *want to accompany you!* ".

I always had facilities to get visas, and I sent the list of people who were going to come, and they all got their visas.

Because of the preparation for the wedding, Mylène didn't see any of that, but it was a real struggle.

Christian's mother, in the end, did not want to come but delegated a woman from her family to replace her.

We arrived in South Africa. It was the wedding day, and there was a limousine to take us to the church. It was the first time I got into a limousine, and I was very moved.

Ah, children... I have had fights, which have made me cry many times.

Mylène's marriage pronounced, and we went home.
I had to go to Marika!

MARIKA...

Marika fell ill: she couldn't see anything. His eyes no longer worked. His eyes were white. I was scared.

I prayed, prayed, but one day, I decided to go see the doctor who prescribed me medication... that a child could not take! On paper, she even risked death! And it seemed to have nothing to do with what she had. I didn't give it to him.

I had connections, and I went to see a white doctor. A psychiatrist, a lady, who, after examining her, gave her vitamins.

And his eyesight returned to normal.

She just lacked vitamins...

And, much later, she got married to Joël.

Joël was part of President Kabila's circle of advisors. He was a director of something and had a bodyguard who opened the door of his car for him when he got in.

At her wedding, the bodyguard was still there. This impressed everyone. And that impressed my daughter.

But as Marika loved Joël, and as Joël loved Marika, the marriage was made.

Second marriage! But now it was necessary to continue on the path and marry Yves.

YVES – III – GREAT BRITAIN

A bad memory is when I managed to leave for London, two or three years after my "beating."

Since the sequence with the military, I didn't leave the house. To get the passport, the visa, the process is long, too. With all this, I damaged my schooling: I no longer went to school, because I was afraid to go out. I was traumatized.

One day, Dad, who initially didn't want me to go abroad, came to my room and said, "I can see you're scared. And I can see what was done to you," and it hurt me. "So, I make the decision: you leave!"

I was twenty years old, and I left all my family and friends there to go to a country where I knew neither the system nor the "how it works"... When I got on the plane, I didn't know if it was a goodbye or a farewell either. But because I believed in myself, I didn't look back, I got on the plane and left.

Yves was already in England. Sandy was in Cape Town, South Africa. They had known each other since school.

So I went to South Africa to visit Sandy, I had this grace.

> *One day, I called them, in the Congo: I told my mother that I was going to marry my girlfriend, who was my neighbor in the neighborhood. She thought I was an adventurer. They were surprised because it had been a long time since I had given any news.*
>
> *We saw each other again in South Africa. I felt great joy to see mom and dad again, together, at my wedding.*
>
> *It was this joy that I wanted to give him as a gift at that moment. I had to do that!*

Finally, Yves asked his dad to go and endow Sandy. It was the family that endowed it, I couldn't do it anymore.

Yves had never travelled, only to England. So, I had to organize everything from the Congo. Yves left London for South Africa via Brazzaville, and we left Kinshasa.

> *I remember Yves' wedding. At home, there was nothing left. Really nothing. And dad said to me, "You're not going to stay, we'll all go to Yves' wedding." He did everything: I could see how he did it. To the point of selling the car so that I too could go to South Africa. Mom was already gone. One morning, we left for the airport. On the plane, there was a gentleman I didn't know. He asked me:*
>
> *— "You're going to South Africa, but where are you from?"*
>
> *— "I come from Kinshasa, from La Gombé."*
>
> *He talks to me as if he knew me.*
>
> *When I arrived in Johannesburg, Dad told me to wait to get the tickets to Cape Town. I hear that luggage is "above." I ask, I ask... Finally, I go upstairs, and I tell myself that dad will come and get me here. I wait for the luggage: thirty minutes, an hour, two hours...*
>
> *I'm starting to get worried; I was scared. I was a child, I didn't have a phone like I do today, in a country I didn't know... I didn't have any money, either... I didn't know how to look for my parents. And I was crying and praying...*
>
> *Finally, the gentleman who was talking to me on the plane came to see me:*
>
> *"Why are you crying?"*
>
> *"I don't have my dad: he went to buy tickets..." »*

> *He got up, asked where the ticket office was to buy tickets, and left. And in turn, he dragged his feet...*
>
> *And suddenly, I saw Dad, and I was very happy to see him! And we went to the wedding: it was the first time for many things.*

They got married in the Anglican Church, as Yves was English, and everything went very well. It was moving.

Afterwards, Yves returned while Sandy stayed in South Africa before joining her family in Congo.

They were separated for a long time: it was complicated for the visa. It took her six months before she was able to join him.

MYLÈNE – I – GREAT BRITAIN

> *I was already in London, until my father died. I regretted his death very much, but it took me ten years to forgive him afterwards.*
>
> *It took me a while to heal. I prayed morning, noon, and night to tell him, in his grave, that I forgave him for what he had done.*
>
> *I ended up freeing myself completely from it, and I am at peace today. Even if I still don't understand where this story of beating a woman comes from.*
>
> *Seeing what I had seen was too much: a trauma that gnawed at me for years.*
>
> *There was too much male domination, and mom had to find a way to deal with it herself.*

YVES – III – GREAT BRITAIN

> *On my wedding night, Dad told me that he was tired. He also told me: "If you hear that I am dead, you don't go back, continue with your wife."*
>
> *Two years later, when I flew back to England from a holiday in South Africa, everything went well, but as soon as I landed, my phone rang. Marika said to me: "Daddy is dead!"*

> *I couldn't go back, so I went home. I called Mom, and she told me not to come.*
>
> *She was the one who came sometime later. I wanted her to stay, but she didn't want to because of the English.*
>
> *She left for Paris. I went to see her twice, and it made me as happy as it worried me: I felt she was very lonely. And it hurt me. There was something abnormal.*

MÉLISSA – IV – USA

> *In 2011, I received a call in the morning from Marika telling me to come and find her: dad had just had a stroke.*
> *Three days later, the parents were transferred from Ngaliema to La Gombé because his father's condition was not improving. He stayed there for the week, but this time mom wasn't alone: there were women who spent the night outside praying with mom to get daddy healed.*
>
> *In the hospital hall, Mom says to me: "Your daddy doesn't stop insulting me!"*
> *I ask, "Why?"*
> *She says, "I don't know!"*
> *Then she adds: "It's the devil in him. It's not him! We will pray for him, and he will have his deliverance... »*
> *She adds: "The Holy Spirit is here!"*
> *I have remained until today with boundless admiration for my mother...*

Until Sandy could get out of the country, I had to go to London, so I took a "*leap of faith*," a symbolic act.

I went to see Sandy, and I told her, "*Pack your suitcase, I'll take you to London, by Faith*." She packed her suitcase, put her pyjamas, her clothes, her shoes, everything that could fit in a small suitcase. I said, "*I'm bringing Yves' wife, I'm taking Sandy to her husband's house*."

I went to see Sandy one last time: "*That's it, I'm taking you to London!* and I flew in Sandy's suitcase.

In London, you must speak English. I managed a little, and fortunately, Mylène had come to pick me up with Yves.

"Yves! I brought you your wife!

"What, mamma?" What?

"We're going to your house, and we're dropping Sandy off."

"Where is she?"

"The suitcase is Sandy!"

Mylène takes her car, and we leave for Yves' house. I arrived in his room, and I said:

"Sandy, I'll take you home: soon, you'll see your husband!"

I left the suitcase there, and we went to Mylène's.

MYLÈNE – I – GREAT BRITAIN

> *In the end, mom had managed to manage her husband, but I still can't stand to see a couple fighting. I couldn't stand violence.*
>
> *Even today, when I hear a woman crying, it takes me ten seconds to pull myself together because I was traumatized by what I went through. I must reassure myself.*
>
> *I can't stand the screams. I don't know how to have a relationship with someone "in Cree", I can't.*
>
> *Ten years ago, and even five years ago, at night, when I closed my eyes, I heard crying.*
> *It woke me up in a panic, and I had trouble breathing.*
> *I had to heal from that!*

I returned to Congo, but by this time, Sandy had reapplied for her visa.

While she had not been given it for years, she obtained it a few weeks later.

She was able to join Yves. God is good!

MYLÈNE – I – GREAT BRITAIN

> *But all that is in the past: we buried dad with a lot of love. We loved him, we love him, and we will always continue to love him. And in the grave where he is, may the Lord take care of him! We forgive the living and the dead: we cannot remain with such strong grudges.*

Now Melissa was left to marry!

MARIKA – II – CONGO

> *The salon resisted until Daddy's death.*
> *Since the death of our father, we have experienced so many things... Mylène was in Europe, and the one who was close to them was me. I took a lot, and that's why I wouldn't testify to everything I've experienced.*

MELISSA

Meli had other habits. She had many friends... I didn't like it! This gives a bad reputation. So, I would talk to Meli, but she would go for a walk and come home late. I told her dad about it, and he just told her, "*Come on, Meli is going for a walk with your friends!* ".

Where she went, she met Pascal... How? I don't know...

Pascal had lost his wife, with whom he had four children. The cubs had been entrusted to his sister in the United States.

When I first met him, I insulted him and chased him out of my house.

MÉLISSA – IV – USA

> *Dad died on September 6, 2011.*
> *Mamma cried for her husband with all her might*
> *She did not wash or feed herself during the entire month of mourning. And she cut her hair for a year.*
>
> *A month later, she was still sleeping a lot, but getting better and better, and she had regained her calm.*
> *Over time, as the years went by, I understood that her marriage made her unhappy: she loved her husband so much, but unfortunately, she did not receive what she expected.*
>
> *All this is to say that we have a mother who is so brave and strong and protective to the point of forgetting herself. She forgot that her identity is what caused all her suffering.*

But one day, I heard a voice telling me not to "*mistreat Pascal*" and "*to ask him for forgiveness.*"

I was coming back from church, and I saw them both on the side of the road. So, I went to meet them:

"Pascal, pardon me... Really, everything I could say was unfair.

There, Pascal told me that they wanted to continue together and that they had come to agree on marriage.

Pascal had a good salary, so he organized everything in a large prestigious hotel. Meli looked very beautiful in a beautiful dress. Pascal's family had come from the United States and Belgium to attend the ceremony.

I had married Meli!

But then, my sisters-in-law launched a battle of rumors and bad tongues. It was painful, but prayer had become my meal.

Like my twin: all these marriages put her in a bad mood. She was invited, but you felt... My children know this well... What can such an attitude correspond to?

MÉLISSA – IV – USA

> *Mom had a small car that Mylène and her husband had bought her when she had lost everything. That Mylène had given her this car made her proud... Despite the problems she had, she continued to take care of herself. I admire my mother: she passed on her values to me... And above all, never let anyone tell you who you are!*
>
> *When I saw mom being beaten and insulted, when I saw how she was denigrated by the person who was supposed to love her... I had a feeling of anger that, during all this time, I had to stifle and that I continue to suffocate.*
>
> *Mylène gone, Yves gone, Marika married, so left the house, only me and Claudia were left. But she was very small.*
> *I didn't want to be there! I couldn't look my mother's suffering in the eye without being able to do nothing... Before dad died, he had calmed down a little, but mom told me that dad was insulting him, for nothing... I understand his pain, his pain in continuing, until God decided to take daddy.*

Today, it's over, and Meli is in the United States.

And after my husband's death, Marika said to me: "*You, Mom, are not going to stay in this country!* ".

I replied: "*Your father is dead. So, I'm going to change, I'm probably going to take a blank. A white man, not a black man.*" I used to say that all the time...

MYLÈNE – I – GREAT BRITAIN

> *I had my trauma, Mélissa and Yves, too. In his life as a couple, my brother experienced a reflection of that. I had to go to him and talk to him. I also spoke with Sandy, his wife, and I told her: "You can always call the police!"*
> *He changed afterwards.*
>
> *This trauma pushes you to have certain relationships with each other, which are just the result of "how you grew up" in your parents' house.*
>
> *Not all Africans are like dad, and his family bond, of course. But with all my uncles, dad's brothers, it was the same violence: they beat their wives and in a savage way. One of them divorced barely a year after being married. He, too, beat his wife, savagely. It wasn't pretty.*

LA FRANCE...

I have visited many countries.
We had gone to Belgium for a holiday...
We had gone to see the tomb of a local saint: Brother Mutien Marie Wiaux[36], in Malonne.

Belgium, I didn't like it too much...

My daughter lives in London, but there's the problem of English: it's complicated!
Like America, with my other daughter.
The violence in the Congo led me to travel perhaps to protect me, the Visionary sent me to the United States.

But there is no question of returning to Congo. My successes had provoked jealousy: the Visionary was in a state

---

[36] Beatified in October 1977 by Pope Paul VI

of disarray, and his wife was shouting everywhere, "*What's going on with Mado?* ". She came to her church on Sundays and could see that there was "*something more.*" She didn't understand and told lies.

At that time, my passport was full of visas.
I went to London to see my children. But since I don't know English, I didn't like the city. I didn't feel any particular attraction.

When I discovered France, I immediately liked it!

MYLÈNE – I – GREAT BRITAIN

> *One day, you'll have to go back to Congo, at least for a week. You have nothing to lose and much to gain in tranquility. This is very important because you have to liberate souls there, and you have to free yourself. You have so many secrets in your heart that you have to go back there to heal. It will undoubtedly be very strong. There are so many memories and things left unsaid.*
>
> *Apart from you, the person who suffered the most was probably Marika, because she stayed there. She lived and spent in these places that were the family's places. But today, Marika is doing well and living well, too! You will have to stop worrying about it! And we are all well: my brother and his wife, my sisters, and their husbands.*
>
> *For me, coming back to the Congo cured me: I walked down certain avenues, with the memory of "I've already been here." I'm fifty-two years old today, and I've decided to stop crying.*
>
> *I walked and it did me good! I saw that things had changed!*

"Pastor Mado"
© Marie-Madeleine Kabange Ngoie

Marie-Madeleine, her husband Yvon, and their 4 children
© Marie-Madeleine Kabange Ngoie

PART 2: FRANCE

I was a widow, my husband having died in September 2011 of a stroke, and I was alone. So, why not go to France?

In Congo, I was harassed by my in-laws and my neighbors: everyone wanted my house back, to chase me out of my home.

The four of them came, while I was crying and praying with mothers from the Church. They wanted to make me leave and make me obey the Custom.

MYLÈNE – I – GREAT BRITAIN

> *When I meet someone from the family, I rectify what they tell me, I stay positive.*
>
> *Some didn't approve of what dad was doing to you, even if they never came to tell you. There are still a lot of prejudices. They don't know, anyway, what made you start to get into a fight. Cousins, especially: "Mama Mado? She's fine? After everything she has been through… »*
>
> *When dad went out to give his view of the facts, no one in our house knew what he was saying about mom.*
>
> *I told some that you had your life, that you had someone in your life, and that you were making your life, now, that you had not stayed in the past, that you were moving forward.*

But where to go? It was complicated, it was strong, and I risked death. I was left to myself.

Custom… The custom among Africans is that if the husband dies, the family of the deceased takes everything! And his wife is part of the legacy[37]!

---

[37] A custom, originating from the Old Testament, called the "levirate" (from the Latin "*levir*", "the husband's brother"), forbidden in several countries, but still authorized, nowadays, in some West African countries, and tolerated in Congo. "Renouncing the levirate" is possible, according to

She must marry one of the dead man's brothers, to ensure the continuity of the lineage, and his children become his children. I was left with Claudia, who, during this period of mourning, was with her natural mother, Gui-Gui. Otherwise, they would have taken it from me, too.

I didn't like it, but custom leaves no choice: I had no other options. I had to find a solution: leave everything behind and leave, quickly!

CLAUDIA – V – CONGO

> *You are a very strong person, mother, courageous, tolerant, patient. I saw a lot of things when I was in La Gombé, but I was only a child. But what really broke me was your departure. When Papa Yvon died, I was at my Mama Gui-Gui's house. I really didn't know how to cry. A few months later, my mother Gui-Gui died, too. So, I went back to La Gombé. I felt loved, despite the death of dear, important loved ones. I had lost my dad, then my mom, but I felt loved, in your house where I was comfortable.*
>
> *In the street, on my way back from school, I was walking with my classmates. That's what we call school friends. But walking down the street, I was a little scared. And you were waiting for me outside and worried. You were afraid for me. Since your departure, until today, I have no one to worry about my fate.*
>
> *When you went to France, you shattered my dreams. You have shattered my childhood. You have broken my thoughts; you have broken everything.*
>
> *When you have parents next door, the father looks after his children, and so does the mother... We have certain stupidities that we limit ourselves to doing: "if I do this, mom will get angry..." ». Friends can push you, but even if she's not around, or if she finds out, she'll be really furious with me. And your brain tells you "If you do this, it will be really complicated".*
> *And I had no one left to take care of me.*
> *You left, and I stayed, suffering.*

another custom, but does not solve all the problems of the widow who often has to abandon everything and leave the village and the region.

The Church was looking for someone to animate the Church in Paris. I accepted. They managed to send me away, paying me for the ticket, and I left without telling anyone, to avoid problems. I only took a suitcase and my Bible. Everything remained on site. I don't know what happened to it... I did this for the children, so that they could live freely. That was my vision: that they study up to university, that they get married.

When I left Congo, I had only one word, for my husband's family: "I forgive you! You don't respond to evil with evil: God will take care of you! »

When I arrived in France, I was called "*Marie-Madeleine*", and no longer "*Mado*" or simply "*Madeleine*", so I was happy. When I am called Mary Magdalene, I feel within me like oil entering my heart. I feel peace within me: the name of Mary Magdalene is sacred!

I wanted to be independent, but here too, I was blocked a lot. As I didn't know anything, they played with me.

I wanted a small place to be able to work and prepare my interventions. But each time, it was the same serenade: "*no, you don't have papers, we're going to expel you if you show yourself too much*"...

CLAUDIA – V – CONGO

> *So, I went to Melissa's house. But it was complicated. I didn't know, for example, how to pay for water? What do we do to buy food? I was really sheltered from wants, but it was short-lived.*
>
> *When Melissa left to give birth, I was still alone. So, I went to see one of my aunts. And that's when I learned that you must go and get food, that running water has to be paid for. She didn't have much, even though she was working. She had a minimal salary, and many children. She brought food in the evening, but in the morning, we had to make do. At lunchtime, the same if you were hungry, you had to make do.*
>
> *It was at that time that I understood that life was hard. And that I started crying.*
>
> *Papa Yvon didn't want me to cry. He didn't want to see a single tear on my cheek. He didn't want to see me suffer. I*

> *must have been thirteen, but he took me like a child of six months, spoiled, rocked, pampered. And I started crying for Daddy Yvon...*
>
> *When Mama Mado was there, she told me "No, not Sunday plates", and I had learned to wash plates. She also taught me how to make rice. I learned a lot of things, such as doing the Sunday "illumination." I learned to work. And maybe if she had been there, I wouldn't have experienced what I did.*
>
> *So, I cried for Papa Yvon, Mama Gui-Gui, Mama Mado, and even Melissa, who stayed. And in his house, I ate well, I slept well, I lived well, in good conditions.*
> *But she was also gone, and everything had become complicated. And I grew up like that, without living well, even if I ended up finding it normal.*
> *Simple things became complicated, for example the toilets. I was used to sitting on the tank, and then I moved on to the "hole".*

So, I let myself be done... I was scared. The fear of expulsion, the fear because I had no one to confide in: alone, I could do nothing. The Church Visionary told me, "*No, we can't get you papers,*" and the Church people added, "*We can't!* ".

I'm versatile, though, and I know how to do a lot of things. But they told me "You *don't have papers, you don't work!* without showing me what to do to get it. So, they did with me what they wanted. I went to immigration alone, alone. And I didn't know what to do and say: they left me in nothingness, just like that!

And in Paris, in the churches, the same thing happened as in the Congo: people came to me, and put money in my Bible, to thank me. At the end of that first sermon, there was €1,700 in my Bible. So, I took €600, which I kept for myself, to live, and I gave the rest to the Church. They sent part of it to Kinshasa. But that I took a little money to live on caused them problems, and it was a debate.

I continued, with the same success. There were trances, healings, and when I left the church, people followed me.

You wanted to defend yourself, as a woman, you wanted to exist, to save your life. And your way of doing it, because you were in front of a man who was beating you, was to go there. You couldn't do anything else: the Bible wasn't enough. Neither does your voice. At that time, you no longer owned anything: you were one hundred percent dependent on your husband. You weren't alive, so you had to get out of there, it was quite normal.

Like many women, you lived in a "marital prison", and you had no voice. The Book, the Bible, can help to get out of it, but it does not take the place of the one who must act.

Once, you jumped from the balcony of your room that led to the main exit: dad was beating you, and probably he was suffocating you! You decided to jump, and it was on the second level.

One time I heard crying during the night, and I woke up to see what it was... You were crying, I don't know why! I stayed by your side... In the morning, your mouth was swollen.
"Mom, why are you like that?"
She replied: "I pierced a button..." »
It wasn't true: Daddy had hit her again.

I studied law in Congo, and my motivation was born because I saw a mother who was beaten, and who didn't even know how to talk about it. So, I studied law to defend women, and to give them a voice. I said "no, I have to speak for her!" because it was too much!
We were children, we couldn't do anything, and she, who was supposed to protect us, couldn't do anything either.

In winter, in France, I'm not used to it. I'm cold... I am alone, without friends, without papers. I'm afraid of the slightest control. I'm afraid of losing my job, that I'll be deported, but I have no choice: they give me little, a few euros, but that's all I have.

One day, it was slippery, and I wanted to take my bus. I fell, and I hurt myself. I didn't say anything, and I went to work until the evening...

The Church was blocking me. It hurt me a lot, but I ended up leaving her. I was disappointed, not by just one church, but by the four I attended in France. All that jealousy eventually turned into harassment, so I was crying all the time... it wasn't right... Each time, I worked hard, and they gave me a few euros to survive. In Chelles, they gave me nothing.

A shepherd's wife ended up being embarrassed by my closeness to her husband. She was multiplying her thoughts.

One day, a woman came to me and said "*your wig smells like poop!* ". She was criticizing my outfit. I didn't understand I'm clean, and I dress normally! I buy the clothes that others buy. I didn't have a lot of money, they didn't pay me, but I did what I could. I left.

At the time, I was living in Bondy, with a woman who took pity on me and sent me to the Church of Lognes.

In Lognes, they gave me two hundred euros, but they quickly decreased to one hundred euros. I couldn't do anything with it, nor could I say anything either.

I ended up leaving, and I was hosted by a thirty-year-old woman in Nanterre. But I cried all the time.

In France, I was suffering: my colleagues told me that people didn't like me anymore. It made me cry: I had no one, in France, I had no friends. My daughter Mylène started to have Missions everywhere and disappeared for weeks.

I ended up talking to the Pastor about it. He had commercial premises in Stains, with a tenant who did not pay his rent. He ended up leaving, and I took his place.

The state wanted to expel everyone[38], but I stayed. I set up a small office and a bedroom.

The Pastor was kind to me, and he promised to declare myself... but he did nothing.

---

[38] It was an unsanitary squat...

Everyone was nice to me, even the police, and they didn't kick me out right away.

The first thing I did in Stains was to celebrate a wedding. I was in pastoral dress, and it was good.

They also sent me to preach in the provinces, for three days in a hotel.

After Stains, in Bondy, Madeleine, a widow, rented me a room for €400. My children paid every month. But there was no heating, and in winter I slept with the raincoat and thick socks.

It was she, my landlady, who asked the Pastor of Lognes to help me. I don't know what she told him, but he gave me fifty euros to help me.

One day, she invited me to her church. And the pastor asked me if we could work together. He was married to a French woman. She welcomed me well, at first.

In Lognes, I went all the time to preach with the Visionary. One day, he said to me, "*Pastor Mado, God tells me that you have a gift, you must have a ministry!* ". I replied, "*God is not a confusionist! And every time I preach, people follow me! I have worked to speak normally, with words that everyone understands, and I am telling the truth.*" When I preach, I remain natural.

He enjoyed it, but when he preached, it was "*something else*": he put theology in his French, and spoke well, too well for people.

I started preaching, and here too, very quickly, the church was filled. People came, confided in each other, I strengthened them, and it made them feel good.

The faithful came to find peace, but when they left the Church, there were again condemnations and "*God told me! God told me!* ".

I was preparing the ceremonies, and it was there that a faithful, Brother Richard, became attached to me.

He helped me a little, administratively, on what I had to do to get my papers, but it didn't come to fruition.

The Pastor had studied theologically, and he spoke French well. But the words were those of the university.
When I stood on the pulpit, he stood up and chanted, "*Pastor Mado!* ". When I speak, people listen and I preach them a living Bible, daily. When I read the Bible, I read it differently: I want to understand where it happened, how, why? So, when I preach, I visualize the scenes.

Other pastors came from Belgium to see what I was doing, and why the Church was filling up a little more each time.

I worked a lot, but I wasn't paid. I held vigils, did work in the Church, but that did not prevent jealousy from striking again. The pastor didn't want people to come and talk to me directly, out of his presence.

Little by little, the pastor began to preach as if he were preaching to me. I didn't like it. One day, I got angry, and I shouted in the church, "*No, Pastor, you don't know me!* ". I lost my temper! It was terrible...
But since then, I prefer to say that I prophesy in myself, for myself. No longer in public.

I worked in four churches, in all: instead of helping me to develop, they kept me prisoner and prevented me from progressing. The four of them treated me like an object, practical, cheap, efficient. And jealousy was everywhere.
All the while, my children have been forced to send me money... They never left me. I owe them a lot.

CLAUDIA – V – CONGO

I was forced to adapt, because I had no source of income, I had nothing of my own. And I was pregnant. Having the father of my child on the phone was complicated, still problems.

I had no more support... My mother, whom I loved, Mama Mado, had left me, probably because she was angry with me.

> *She didn't know that she was slowly killing me. To whom could I explain that I was suffering? Mama Mado wasn't there, and Melissa was furious with me.*
>
> *And then there was Marika.*
> *Once, she came to the house, and said to me "you don't study?" I told him that it was due to a lack of resources. So, she told me "At least you have to graduate!" And out of her own pocket, she paid for my studies.*
> *I can only be grateful to him.*
>
> *We don't really talk with Marika. I find it a little... Complicated! I don't know how to describe it.*
> *She is complicated, but she is someone who, in case of a problem, is always present and always reaches out her hand. She is always willing to help. We are not perfect, each of us has flaws. I have flaws, and I make efforts to understand her and adapt, but I am grateful to her first and foremost.*

WORK – UNDECLARED – WITH A DOCTOR...

I eventually found work with a doctor, but he couldn't hire me.

In fact, with all my worries – today we would talk about stress – my health was deteriorating, and I had to go to a general practitioner, a Moroccan. I told him everything, and he referred me to a psychiatrist colleague in Drancy, who needed an assistant.

But then again, I was "*almost*" a volunteer. I think he felt sorry for me... He gave me €10 per hour of work. But as every time I got a residence receipt, he was marked "*without work permit*", he said that he could not hire me and declare me. He insisted and specified that "*if the prefecture agreed*", he would declare to me, but that he "*could not do anything more*". I was doing a good job, so he kept me. And it went on for years: eight years... He was confident. Until Covid...

ARRIVAL IN ÉVRY

A shepherd's wife, jealous, was always harassing me, and I had tears in my eyes all the time. I had to leave.

It was the wife of the Pastor of Lognes, who found a solution: she had an apartment to rent, a studio, and she offered it to me. It was far from Chelles, in Évry.

MÉLISSA – IV – USA

> *Mother, when she arrived in France, perhaps without knowing it, without being aware of it, she continued in that spirit: a fighter! At a high level!*
> *This is what makes him proud, what makes him strong! She is a brave and strong woman.*

That's how I ended up in Évry.

And in Évry, after the lockdown, to keep myself busy and get out of my loneliness, I ended up meeting the "*Generation II Citizenship Integration*" Association, which welcomed me, and I found peace.

The director, Mrs. Aisseta Cissé[39], is good, with a heart, and I am grateful to her, until today. She did me a lot of good, I will never forget her.

When I arrived, I went to see her, and I told her: "*I want to accompany you in your task*". She trusted me, and immediately gave me a group of newcomers who wanted to learn French. And, as a volunteer, I have been since 2020.

One morning, as it was very cold, Mrs. Cissé gave me a blanket. Very hot, very thick, it must have been very expensive... I cried all night. But for this grace, Madame Cissé is in my heart: I adopted her.

My learners focus on French, but also on their ability to integrate into society, to be autonomous in daily life.

In fact, we all accompany each other and exchange experiences, and that also does me a lot of good.

From the beginning, all the learners have marked me, and sometimes I come across some in the street who jump on my neck saying "*thank you!* ". And their children jump on my

---

[39] This woman has lived a remarkable career that it would take too long to detail here. Knight of the Legion of Honor, she will be decorated with the Medal of Children and Families in March 2024 at the UDAF 91 (Departmental Union of Family Associations of Essonne).

neck calling me "*mama*". There are different nationalities, and they are good: they want to get by! Ukrainians, Russians, Turks... A Portuguese psychologist, who could not find a job in France: she is now settled and married to a Frenchman. We send each other text messages regularly.

I appreciate the values and actions of "*Generation II Citizenship and Integration*", which include all members of the same family, men, women, children.

Danièle Girondin, its president, is a wise person and a philosopher. She gives words of wisdom that give life back to those who listen to her. For me, she made me want to stay upright: "*If you fall off your bike, are you going to stand there, crying? No, you shake off the dust and get back on your bike to reach your destination.*"

Often, when I'm not well, I go and sit under a tree in the park next to my house and think about the words that are being spoken. I was doing that too, in Congo. Give yourself time to think we should do this more often!

The Association is better than a church: it doesn't think for us, it helps us integrate, it restores confidence, which the churches have never done for me. It also helps to know and understand the Values of the Republic, to orient oneself, to conceive what is possible to do or not to do.

RETURN TO THE CATHOLIC CHURCH

Since my arrival in Évry, I have been going to the Catholic Church, to the cathedral of Évry.

It was a terrible time, and in my head, everything was rushing. Why am I all alone? What for? I don't even have any papers. I spent a lot of time in the pastor's church, and he didn't help me. He said that "*it was complicated*" for the papers. Same for the doctor...

When I went to see a Catholic priest to go to confession, he told me in turn, "*It will be difficult to get your papers.*"

And instead of giving me back my faith, with reassuring words like "*it's going to be okay!* ", it has dented my morale.

I was a loyal normal, though! I hadn't done anything to deserve this! God does not excommunicate his children. My heart doesn't reproach me for anything. I behave normally. I have not committed adultery, I have not blasphemed, and I continue to live my life as a Christian. This is my personal faith: Christianity is individual!

"God told me"?

And I no longer agree with the "*God told me* "That I used to hear. I can't stand the "*Me, my church, Me!* of the preachers. It's their money, above all. And I refuse to have hands laid on me, and all these rituals. I decided to work inside myself because I had to be clean inside.

YVES – III – GREAT BRITAIN

> *My mother, she prayed to God all her life. Even if it didn't always do him good. "Pray for me, pray for us... ».*
>
> *I realize that today, without God, I am nothing. Mom gave me a lot. She also gave me a Bible when I was twelve, and I still have it. It is with it that I find my strength and recharge my batteries: I always connect it as if it were new. And I face life with her, as my mother taught me.*
>
> *Of all that I have seen today, I want peace at home. What is your contribution on earth? What's your story? So, we might as well develop the positive in our lives!*

This examination of conscience led me to seek a better understanding of the Bible: it is a course of action even if it is a double-edged sword.

With the Bible, you can also do harm. If *"God said"* to kill, you kill!
But God never said that! The Bible is love. God speaks to us above all of love. But how can I do good?

So, I began to think: if I preach about love, people are happy, and don't think about their problems anymore.

It is only today, with the age I am, that I understand that Christianity is not just a building. Christianity is in the heart, and it is love. So, I'm talking about love, not about the church.

The stories of "*God Told Me*", "*The Sorcerers Who...*" "*Your father told me...*" I don't want it anymore! All this, I cannot continue.

MÉLISSA – IV – USA

> *An anecdote? I was already married in Kinshasa. One evening, I was invited to a wedding at a cousin's house on my father's side.*
>
> *Dad was no longer there. He was already dead, in fact.*
>
> *I was with my husband, and there was a gentleman, short in stature, and bald like that, who kept staring at me. He looked at me insistently, and it became embarrassing.*
>
> *At one point, I go to the buffet to help myself to food, and there, he comes to me:*
>
> *"Are you the twins' daughter?"*
>
> *I said to him:*
>
> *"There are several twins!"*
>
> *"No, the Lubumbashi twins!"*
>
> *My husband, relieved, rushes over:*
>
> *"Yes, yes, yes! It's her!*
>
> *"Oh my, you look like your mother!" They were called "the Cleopatras", so beautiful were they! They were so magnificent that wherever they went, in Lubumbashi, they could not remain unnoticed.*
>
> *And this gentleman identified me like this, years later...*

Every morning, I went to the cathedral, before going to the association for my volunteer work. And someone said to me: "*Can you do the reading?* ". I answer "*yes*"!

I read it, and I did it so well that day, that the priest who officiated said to me, "*You're going to do it now!* ".

One day when I was in the pulpit here in the cathedral, I took the Bible, and I began by saying, "Reading according to the Holy Father..." ». And someone interrupts me: "*No, no! It's not like that!* ". Everyone was stunned, even the father. I was scared and wondered what was going on.

When I got home, I was sick, I had a stomachache.

I stayed at home for a long time, to avoid participating in the reading.

Later, I decided to go back to the cathedral. I arrived around eleven o'clock – the readings had already been done – and it was clear in my head: the church is in me!

I have been a widow for fourteen years since my husband died. And in all this time, I never accepted that a man touches my body. It is sacred, reserved for the Lord. I'm a believer, and I believe in myself, as I believe in God, and I believe in what my mind tells me.

And now, I see that a person has come to me, just like that, has fallen from Heaven and opened all the doors that I had double locked.

I accepted, my body accepted, my mind accepted.

Before that, a few months ago, I knew this was going to happen.

I give catechism classes, and we went to the provinces, to Normandy. There were many bishops gathered[40]. And with the catechumens, we had to reflect on sin.

In this old church, there were bishops everywhere. We could go to confession, but I wondered what to say to them.

A companion told me that he was going to do it, so I went ahead and went to see one of the bishops: I told him about my story.

"I've been alone for thirteen years; I've been a widow. I remained faithful to my husband, and I got married at eighteen. I had friends to talk to, but I didn't give away my body. No one can really believe what I say, but it's my heart, and I have my conscience on my side. I'm looking for a friend now, but I'm hesitant. »

---

[40] If there were a few bishops, the priests were in the majority in the assembly.

Then the bishop said to me, "*What is sin?* ". He explains to me that locked in my straitjacket of belief; I was hurting myself more than anything else. He gave me prayers to say and set me free. He even added: "*Do you see all these women and men around us? They are religiously married, but why do they come to confession? So, free yourself! The sin is to be alone: find a companion! I set you free!* »

With the blessing of the bishop, I was very happy. And it was just a few months later that our story began.

I didn't yet know this man who became my friend, my companion, I didn't even expect it.

MYLÈNE – I – GREAT BRITAIN

> *You have not yet stopped praying for me, Mother, and you already have grandchildren for whom you continue the chain of prayer. Three or four years ago, my concern was your recovery. I teach these things and then I realize that my mother suffered more than I should. How do we heal her morally, emotionally, spiritually? Because it's a wound, and it hurts!*
>
> *I carried this burden through prayer for two years.*
>
> *I don't know how you manage to live with a man again. Alan? He's an Angel!*
>
> *If you manage to be honest with your partner, if he has a lot of patience and love, it will work.*

The only thing I told myself, since I've been in France, is that I wanted to live with a white man. A "*white French*". Not for the papers, but for life.

Even before that, I had tried Facebook, but the relationship was distant, distant. One of my contacts was more than three hundred kilometers away. He suggested that we see each other once a month, with words that I didn't understand. My body was sacred, anyway.

When I met Alain, it was different: I had the bishop's permission! Alain has become my partner, and we do each other good, we help each other: I'm happy about that!

MYLÈNE – I – GREAT BRITAIN

> *Today, I have fought, and because I teach, I preach about reconciling families, healing broken hearts. And in the process of teaching, I went through my own deliverance, and eventually, my healing. In the Church, I have children who have this kind of problem in their own homes whom I ask to talk about it. It's a strong fight.*

MÉLISSA – IV – USA

> *Today, I am proud to say that my mother is a fighter.*
> *I always take it as an example.*
> *A strong, independent woman, knowing where she is going and what she wants without being influenced by anything. She has the Spirit God at her side who makes her even stronger.*
> *She often said to me: "My husband is Jesus!" I didn't understand at the time, but today I think it was just to tell us: "I have dedicated my life to God and only He will take care of you and the rest".*

I continue with the "*Generation II Citizenship Integration*" Association: learners come and go. Armenians, Ukrainians, Russians, North Africans, they arrive with the desire to speak better to find work. After a few months, they leave happy, and succeed, all of them!

I tell them, moreover, to remain optimistic, that it will be fine, that everything will be fine. And I ask them to continue to learn, by following the news, the news, on television and on the radio.

In four years, what has changed a little are the priorities: for example, it is important today to learn the Marseillaise. It's not in the churches that they teach it.

I did an internship on secularism and the values of the Republic, and I now understand my rights better. What I can do and what I can't do. It is not the churches that allow you to learn all this. Praying for people is good, holding vigils is good, but when you get home, what's left of it? The association works on the daily, the concrete, and makes learners autonomous. Some go on to join preparatory courses and apply to Science Po. Enough to applaud, and cry with happiness at their success!

Mrs. Cissé helped me transform my residence permit with the mention "authorizes its holder to work", which gave me the right to the CMU, the Complementary Health Solidarity. I also received a lot of training.

MYLÈNE – I – GREAT BRITAIN

> *Not long ago, a white man, a Dutchman, who was invited to a demonstration, said to me, "Will you be able to say hello to your mother for me? Your mother is a real servant of God. She educated you and that's why you are the way you are: she gave you a good education that you gave to your children. Your way of being, of seeing things, reflects that. She is a woman of the spirit, and she has transferred that spirit to you! ». A white man I didn't know who, a priori, doesn't know you.*
>
> *I'm very tired. I'm not the type of person who spreads out on social media: I just need to take a step back, take care of my family and my health.*
> *I understand a lot of things today, because I've grown old, because I've gotten married, because I have children.*
> *I have given a lot, I have given a lot to people, and I need to rest now. I must find other ways of acting and working.*
>
> *I have seen far too many things in the hearts of Africans. I don't want to work with them anymore: the Lord opens other doors for me, other horizons. I have international interviews.*

MARIKA – II – CONGO

> *A lot has changed today, and we have become accustomed to another life, the one we have adopted.*
> *Our parents didn't raise us like Africans, and we grew up with a European culture. We had the habits and customs of Africa, where we do not accept this, where we do not tolerate that, but the will of Europe, where we want this and that. In the neighborhood, we were called "whites with black skin", because we didn't have the same conception of things as the others. And this continues to this day.*
>
> *We have had our ups and downs, but God has given us grace and we have gone through the movements that have taken place in our country.*

We were shaken a lot, we were forced to move my mother very quickly, and we are relieved today to know that she is safe. And our wish is that you will be together for a long time. I wish you all the best.

I am in London today, and I feel good there. I've adapted and I think it's "cool", as they say. God has given me grace and takes care of me until today.

Today, I'm still in London, and my mother is "right across the street", not far away, towards Paris.

I did a lot of jobs in London. I also studied a lot. For ten years, I worked in IT, in the administration of my company. I also spent time with large companies. But I also did electricity.

To this day, I take care of my children, to take them to school and back. If I don't do that, I'll have the government behind me, but in fact, I'm busy while I wait to start my own business.

Nothing to do with what I did before, and on the contrary, a return to my roots: I want to become a sports coach.

My children are grown up today, and I decided to do what my heart has always wanted to do: weight training. With my size, it's still possible. But here, you can't do anything with young people. You must study again and take courses. I finished a few days ago and started working in a gym. Eventually, I plan to open my own gym. From computer science to bodybuilding, it can be surprising, especially since I was good at the former. My wife continues in IT.

Mom, not long ago, I showed a friend a picture of you, from that time and she thought it was me. Like what, I look like you, how beautiful I am like you, and I can only say thank you!

The pain of living with a suffocation, coming from the past, shatters a life and shatters dreams! I adopted a certain character to flee away from my trauma and away from a pain that never ended. I felt guilty that I had never acted: I wanted to protect Mom, but it was too much.

I had to flee, to be away from this pain for fear of committing suicide. I cried for nothing, I was sad for nothing, I was angry for nothing... I didn't want anything. I still have after-effects... My husband, sometimes, doesn't understand me (I hope that if he finds the chance to read this wonderful book, he will understand) ...

My fear of seeing mom one day on the floor, lifeless, turned into anger! What I saw as a child made me very angry, but I pray for it... I don't like to see or feel this anger in me: because of it, I have destroyed and hurt those around me.

That great heart, which she bore everything without saying anything: she passed it on to us!
I often keep my children at the table every night. I insist that we eat as a family because mom did everything to keep us together.

Mom, I've always taken you as an example! Sometimes I am sad, and I cry. Sometimes I get angry and regret never being there when you really needed it! I was barely between ten and eleven years old.
Today, I see you and I'm happy: you have the man who suits you.
When you told me about Alain, I said to myself "Um, okay!" ... But by talking to him, I accepted it because you want it, and I want to see you happy.

It's rare to see a child, raised in a house, who is considered like all children. I really had this chance, this grace, to grow up and be educated by good people.

Too often I have seen grown-ups treat adopted children badly, who are not their own. They are not in the house of mom and dad, but in the house of an aunt, an uncle, a friend. They don't get the right education, they are set apart, and end up on the street.
Me, in the house of La Gombé, I felt at home, at home. I went to good schools, even though there wasn't much money at the time I was born. The French I speak today I owe to my adoptive parents. And the work I do is thanks to the way I speak and write French. I thank my God for putting me in a very good family. It's my mom, and my dad, and I don't know any others.

Madeleine
(70 years old)
© Marie-Madeleine Kabange
Ngoie

Mary Magdalene
(71 years old)
© 2023 Alain Avanthey

Mary Magdalene (72 years old)
© 2024 Alain Avanthey

ALAN

PART 3: THE ADMINISTRATIVE MARATHON

Now, I'm taking back control.

We leave biography to enter the sociological, if not ethnological, reporting of the habits and customs of the French administration of the twenty-first century.

My objective was simple: how to give Mary Magdalene a little security in our "policed" society practicing exclusion? Citizen security, but also, a minimum, financial, social, legal...

She is not the type to twiddle her thumbs, and having regained her self-confidence, she is investing in the Association – of which she has become a member of the board of directors – and in her city. Thus, she was co-opted as a member of the Neighborhood Council and appointed "referent." It also participates in the activities of the Learning City (UNESCO), the Citizens' Assembly (Town Hall), and the Scène Nationale de l'Essonne (SNE). All this while providing French courses to newcomers for the Association. At 72 years old, she can only be a volunteer...

She wants to become French, to stop chasing residence permits and precariousness, but also because she adheres to the Values of the Republic... and that now she has a French "companion"!

I will help him in this: we are a few months away from an electoral race against time that sees the European strengthening of the far right, ordinary racism and xenophobia. If she could become French before that deadline...

I took notes throughout our administrative journey: a long-distance race of more than seven months, and it's not over...

I expected the worst, and I was not disappointed... Not funny this marathon, nothing Olympic... Rather Kafka-esque...

And even then, Mary Magdalene has a residence permit in due form... I can imagine the struggle of the "undocumented"... Farmers are asking for a "simplification" of administrative procedures: I can only agree with them, for the whole country and the sectors!

I'll tell you about the start of the galley... Let's cast off!

THE GENESIS...

Since we have been together, Mary Magdalene has been sleeping safely, with heating I make sure. But I quickly realized that this has not been the case for her for the last thirteen years.

First shock where I wonder!

Why and how was she able to survive all this time, without papers, without her "employers" being subjected to the slightest control that could have immediately changed her situation? How many, in his case, anonymous and hard-working, forced to the limit of slavery?

SHAME AND PRIDE

And I ask her a little more about her state of health: second shock, and that's where it all begins.

I am not hiding anything from you, I am telling you from the outset: I am ashamed of my humanities and my France! What is our motto?

And I'm also proud of them for everything they bring us, compared to the rest of the world, even if it's threatened and called into question. Freedom! Equality! Fraternity?

Pride and shame? It sounds contradictory, but I'm not the only one who feels this way!

At the end of the day, I am left with a grating bitterness that awakens with each teaching position that is eliminated or not replaced, with each public service that closes, with each hospital bed put in the closet, with each nurse who falls into burnout, with each worker who dies on a construction site, with each billion euros diverted to tax havens, and many other dubious choices made in the name of an "accounting logic" that is socially unproductive and destructive of social ties.

Living reality has no use for "accounting logic"! Real people are suffering, real people are hungry, cold or too hot, would like to find a place to live, would like to live a little better, without fear.

GENESIS 2

Let's go back to the story of this genesis: when I met her, Mary Magdalene was suffering from a severe cataract! She had almost become blind, 60%. She could no longer read, type on a keyboard, or move around safely. She said nothing, suffered in silence, and no one had cared about her...

The two implants cost nearly €600, at the expense of the operated patient...

No matter, I convinced her, and a few weeks after the operation, she regained normal vision: 100%, without glasses! Science works miracles... Congratulations to the doctors, surgeons, nurses, and nursing assistants!

Congratulations to her children, who financed the extra cost!

No income, no health insurance, just enough to eat (once his rent and charges are paid, he has between twenty and a hundred euros left per month) and a 100% health insurance card for minimum care, the CSS[41].

I have a pension below the poverty line, and my support can only be limited: we decide to ask for help!

ACRONYMS AND ACRONYMS GALORE...

Hang!
The "Marathon of Acronyms" is taking its marks on the starting line... Top!

---

[41] Complementary health insurance

The acronym [42] is a very French disease! While trying not to be contaminated, I had to learn everything on the job...

Day 1
Visit the city's CCAS, in the town hall. To understand how the system works, to know what it can claim...

The reception official at the town hall was surprised: "What is the CCAS?"
She finally regains her senses, asks a colleague, gives us a waiting number, and declares that "she needs a coffee," which we approve, with a smile...

The CCAS tells us "It's not us" and gives us the number of the CPAM[43] (for help with implants) and the CNAV[44] (for minimum general assistance for retirement, the ASPA[45]).

Day 2
Call to the CPAM – nice welcome – but "it's not us..." ».
We still managed to open an Amélie Account[46] in the process, in two hours of calling, sending and counter-sending various codes by phone and internet... Their "Cat" is an[47] immature AI... or senile, I have a hard time choosing the qualifier!
The struggle, headache, need to breathe...

Some statements by our CCAS interlocutor led us to think that CSS would be a mutual insurance company? We decided to give it a try and send copies of the hospital's invoices to the CPAM.

---

[42] The art of replacing a complicated or compound name with its initials... The National Education, "EN", is breaking all records, but they are not the only ones to play this perverse game...

[43] Primary Health Insurance Fund.

[44] National Old-Age Insurance Fund.

[45] Solidarity Allowance for the Elderly.

[46] The CPAM's digital space with access to individual accounts with the help of an "AmeliBot", a "Chatbot"!

[47] Artificial "intelligence".

Day 3

Call to the CNAV – slow to pick up, on a Friday at 4.45 p.m., but effective for the rest: "You applied for ASPA ten months ago. We replied to you negatively, but it seems that you have not received the document, I am sending it back to you! With it, you can contact the MSA[48] to obtain an SASPA[49]."

D7 (+4 days)

The CNAV was sent by email, four days later, a document dated ... ten months earlier, saying that she "cannot take charge" of Mary Magdalene. But this document is an essential sesame to the rest of the procedure...

D8

An appeal to the "national MSA" refers us to the "MSA Île-de-France", with "not-we-not-we!".

Call to the MSA Île-de-France which, unfriendly and full of condescending "it's not us, sir", ends up sending us away... to the city's CCAS: it is the CCAS that gives the files to be completed to obtain a SASPA!

Day 9

Another visit to the CCAS, in the town hall. The official at the reception does not hesitate, this time, and gives us a call number inviting us to sit in the waiting room.

— "You can't get a SASPA since you haven't had residence permits for 10 years..." »
"Yes, but I have been filing tax returns for twelve years, and I have had residence declarations for as long as that."
"But you have no pay slips?"
— (Me) "Madeleine was swindled by a whole series of people who paid her to the black man... One of them kept it for eight years of work, just like that, promising to declare it: but he never did anything effective! »

---

[48] Agricultural Social Mutuality.
[49] Service de l'Allocation de Solidarité aux Personnes Aînés (Solidarity Allowance for the Elderly).

Consultation with colleagues.

"No, sorry, without residence permits for ten years, we can't do anything..." How old are you, ma'am? »

— "Seventy-one years."

"You don't do them..." But yes, you have been entitled to a pension for sixty-four years."

— (Sighs...) "Great! In the meantime, it doesn't help us for SASPA... »

— "Do you really want to fill out a file? It's long and you need a lot of documents to provide. You will have to return it to us, and we will send it to the MSA... if it is complete."

"Yes, we'll try!"

She rummages through her drawers and hands us a form of several pages...

"Here... If that doesn't work, we'll try the RSA[50]."

"But you tell us that we do not meet the conditions. And why don't we 'try' the RSA now?"

— "You can apply for the RSA if you don't get the SASPA. But it's a long time. »

"The art of going round in circles, then?"

— ...

D16 (+7 days)

Finally, we gathered and scanned all the requested papers... We need to print them now. The association in which Marie-Madeleine volunteers agrees to help her produce these documents.

I look at the CAF website[51] to find out the conditions of the RSA: it's also a failure! It takes five years with a residence permit!

In the thirteen years that Mary Magdalene has been in France, she has never been helped by the people who exploited her. But no one asks us who they are and explains how to throw their dishonesty in their faces!

Hypocrisy reigns: for her to come to work, "they" often paid her a "Navigo Pass", but always without declaring her –

---

[50] Active Solidarity Income.
[51] Family Allowances Fund.

"It's too complicated, we won't make it!" – and without providing her with a pay slip with a minimum income.

She has, therefore, only had a residence permit "with employment" for one year, as for the CSS.

The State, under pressure from the extreme right, in the Senate and the Assembly, is unleashed against "undocumented" people, but no one comes to control the "ordinary" crooks who exploit them! This makes me angry!

However, Mary Magdalene, while understanding that she had been fooled, did not want to file a complaint: "They helped me... I forgive them... ».

FILE SUBMITTED, PAPERWORK COMPLETED?

D20 (+4 days)

I thought the marathon was over, but no, call from the CCAS: there are still papers missing.

Search, scan, print, send.

Expectation!

D36 (+16 days – 1st month)

The Association, seeing that its subsidies are melting, enjoins Marie-Madeleine to pay for her Navigo Pass now. The choices are limited: an annual option... at €120 is the most interesting. It's cheaper than the €80 quarterly that the Association pays, but Marie-Madeleine doesn't have it.

As the request is legitimate, we will nevertheless look for solutions.

We take stock of his papers...

She ordered the renewal of her passport from her embassy, but it takes a long time... Maybe she will get it next year...

Her health insurance card must also be renewed. I helped her make her request on the URSSAF website, and by the way, I updated her address. But very quickly, the account is blocked! What for? I have no idea, no explanation, no contact possible: the telephone lines are "congested"...

We are going to Belgium for a book fair, and I realize that she does not have a European Carte Vitale. I applied for it, and surprise, she passed without a hitch while the renewal of her French Carte Vitale was blocked.

As for the Navigo Pass, the SNCF website is "stuttering"! And, as she had made a first step last year – refused because her address mentioned "hosted by..." – access to a new request is blocked.

It makes me realize that what was an easy thing for her is now becoming an obstacle. For more than ten years, her daughter has put her mother in "accommodation" with her to avoid embarrassing questions about her status. Mary Magdalene was the only occupant, but still officially "housed", which, in the end, prevented any change in the situation.

We call his daughter, in Great Britain, to ask her for a certificate, and we find recent documents, EDF and telephone, where she appears to live in her apartment under her name. Headache, hoping that it works...

D43 (+7 days)

New attempt to relaunch Amélie and renew her Carte Vitale. We have received contradictory messages from the URSSAF: the European card is accepted, and it has received it in its mailbox. But the Amélie account is still blocked for renewal.

After an hour, I start to understand what is going on: the change of address name has blocked the process. We must wait for it to be made official before continuing. The public holidays of the month have disrupted services, no doubt...

J44

Retry: Access is unblocked. But they ask us for a ".JPG format, ID photo. JPEG... "more than 50 KB and less than 2 MB."

I can imagine the dismay of a person who is not used to this kind of language, as I, a photographer, can be.

Especially since the first scanned photo doesn't get through. "Not to the standards requested!" However, it is a ".JPG" file, as recommended.

I try a new attempt: I rename it to. "JPEG", a small nuance of an extra "e", and this time, it passes.

But blocking, immediate: the file does not have the "weight" requested. Once again, I imagine an average interlocutor faced with these dilemmas!

I resize the image, and it passes.

Scan of the Residence permit, with the same constraints: I rename, and I resize.

Request accepted, with an acknowledgement of receipt in the seconds that follow on Mary Magdalene's phone... The card is promised in three weeks in his mailbox.

We blow...

D49 (+5 days)

Marie-Madeleine does receive a letter from the CPAM, but without the card: she asks for a paper passport photo and a new copy of her residence permit... Big anger: we are at three or four uploads on the net, and the account is still blocked, without explanation.

By re-reading the letter, I finally understand that the documents, which I sent to the Amélie account, have the right numerical "weight" but are not... to the right "physical" size. My scan translated my request into an A4 format, enlarging the document to a full page, but the initial request is for a "copy."... on a 1:1 scale on a standard A4 page.

I'm furious: What a waste of time when a simple and clear explanation, or a diagram, would have solved the problem a long time ago!

Is this done on purpose so that the applicants end up giving up? I don't want to fall into the throes of "conspiracy theory," but it's tempting...

D53 (+4 days)

Still no response from CSS regarding the medical costs of the Mary Magdalene operation. CSS is an emergency social security system, but not a real mutual insurance company, as our interlocutor had suggested...

Well, we had to try...

That's it. We have finished composing the SASPA application file.

As a solidarity coach, I am adding a letter for the attention of elected officials, which explains the situation of Marie-Madeleine.

She appears in the photo reports of many official events of the city, accompanied by elected officials, and I slip into the file a "photo album" of these "apparitions" to support my request for support.

We decided to go the following Wednesday to take this file "in person" to the town hall.

SOME PROGRESS: TWO STEPS FORWARD...

D56 (+3 days)

Marie-Madeleine received her new Carte Vitale by post. Once the mechanism was understood and unlocked, it was quickly... But what a hassle!

I reviewed his CV[52] and the cover letter of his SASPA file: some terms, no doubt written in anger, can be misinterpreted, and I change them. We plan to take them to the town hall tomorrow.

J57

This morning, we are submitting the SASPA file for Mary Magdalene to the CCAS.

This time, the young woman who welcomes us does not ask herself what the CCAS is, and it immediately gives us a waiting number.

We are called in a few minutes.

The official who receives us is adorable: she quickly checks that the file is complete and explains the rest to us.

---

[52] Curriculum vitae

The first step is the approval of the file by the mayor. If the latter agrees, the file continues its course towards the specialized fund, the MSA of Lorraine. It will take six to eight months for the company to process the request.

In the meantime, Marie-Madeleine "will receive an acknowledgement of receipt from the mayor" which will allow us to get back to the CAF, which should grant her a temporary RSA aid. If the SASPA application is finally refused by the MSA, the RSA aid will become permanent. At least, that's what is said...

I don't even try to understand the logic of such a sequence and such a delay...

So, everything depends on the mayor now...

In the meantime, we can move on to the next phase: the French naturalization file...

THREE STEPS BACK

D59 (+2 days)

Phone call from the Town Hall, who wants Marie-Madeleine's contact details. I understand that my letter to the elected officials has had its effect, and I have confirmation that the CCAS has not yet forwarded the SASPA request – "it's another service" – submitted two days earlier. The town hall wants to give a hand to a social worker who needs to reach Marie-Madeleine.

An hour later, a phone call from social worker discouraged us: it takes 10 years, "a residence permit with work permit," to obtain the SASPA!

Not at all the discourse of the CCAS but confirmed by a visit to the MSA-SASPA website. It's written in very small letters in the middle of the general conditions of access.

The Social Worker, kind, offers Mary Magdalene the possibility of obtaining food aid... of the Restos du Cœur...

There are people more in need than us, and I can provide meals: we refuse.

I ended up taking the SA on the phone and pointed out that Marie-Madeleine had obtained a work permit, with her residence permit, when she was 70 years old, issued by the prefectural services. This earned him, sometime later, a refusal of a fixed-term contract from the same prefecture... "Because she was too old." At least, that's the version of the person who wanted to hire him.

Kafkaesque, commensurate with the French administration in all its majestic splendour...

The AS nodded, powerless, like us...

I'm still enraged...

But this time, there is probably nothing more to do... Not before two years, with at least five years of residence permit to obtain an RSA. She will be 75 years old... And until then, the law can still change... We lost the race...

There remains the rent assistance...
There remains the heating aid...
There remains the transport aid...
All that remains is naturalization...
The marathon continues...

D64 (+5 days – 2nd month)

This morning, "attempt" to submit the file to the town hall for a Navigo Amethyst Pass. "Attempt" because we were immediately rejected: on the double-sided paper of the "application instructions", there were two lines – very small and quite far apart on the page – which required "proof of housing".

One requires a document that is less than three months old, the other more than a year old. We did have the one for "less than three months" – the last electricity reading – but not the one for " more than a year."

U-turn – on foot – with our file still inactive...

Trouble, when you continue... No one thought of putting this request for a document, basically from the same source, in the same sentence...

D70 (+6 days)

Marie-Madeleine receives in her mailbox a beautiful missive from the Region, signed by the President, telling her that she will receive an energy voucher of €250 that has just been awarded to her... She had made the request "in passing" more than two months ago.

Enough to pay the €120 Navigo fee... and its electricity, of course.

D72 (+2 days)

Here we go again for a trip to the town hall, with a series of papers, to try to have the Amethyst Navigo Pass validated. Marie-Madeleine has been in France for more than ten years, but it was her daughter, initially for practical reasons, who "sheltered" her.

With a certificate in hand, we resubmit the application. The young civil servant smiles: "The file is complete, you will receive your 'Pass Navigo' in your mailbox in about ten days."

This ease disarms me: I expected to have to fight with "pure reason" against "administrative reason," and it seems too easy.

Have the elected representatives unblocked the situation, or is the procedure "normal"? We will probably never know.

To be continued, then...

YOU SALUTE THE PUBLIC IN A LOW VOICE!

D80 (+8 days)

Marie-Madeleine receives her "Navigo Pass," accompanied by a little note from the President of the Region: she has paid the "grant[53]" of unlimited travel in Île-de-France for one year.

---

[53] Tax dating from the thirteenth century and collected in France until 1948, by the municipalities on goods sold in the city.

We still have to find an effective mutual insurance company and, for Marie-Madeleine, to pass the tests to obtain her French nationality. But that's another story...

D110 (+30 days – 3rd month)

In a dramatic turn of events, 52 days after she was submitted, when we had given up all hope, Marie-Madeleine received in her mailbox a receipt for the transmission of her SASPA file to the MSA in Lorraine, which processes the applications.

After discouraging us, the CCAS of the town hall nevertheless communicated the file and obtained the mayor's signature. With this receipt, Marie-Madeleine will be able to make an appointment with the CAF to see what aid she can benefit from.

ROW, THERE WILL ALWAYS BE SOMETHING LEFT!

D112 (+2 days)

We got a telephone appointment with the CAF. Our request is clear: "we have received the receipt from the town hall, we want to get answers from the CAF on the intermediate measures awaiting the response from the MSA." See you in three days...

D115 (+3 days)

What can we say about this meeting? The person does not seem to be aware of the procedural subtleties that link the CAF to the SASPA approach and the MSA...

I am a little annoyed by what still seems to me to be a composed attitude. After ten minutes, I finally took control of the call. As usual, the tone changed: a letter was sent to Mary Magdalene with several commitments, including waiting for the MSA's decision for SASPA and – "... but by the way, is Madame a tenant? ». Yes! « ... So, I will also send him an application form for housing assistance."

My feeling of unease persists once again, we are confronted with what looks like a "posture," which seems negative, at first glance. Should we systematically discourage suitors? But this may only be an opinion fed by fatigue and "administrative allergy," born of my own preconceptions.

D120 (+5 days – 4th month)

Marie-Madeleine finally obtained her Congolese passport. His daughter managed to get him back – somehow – in Congo. He arrived in France with a friend, and we are going to pick him up today on the other side of the Paris region.

It has been more than nine months since she applied for renewal, and after a somewhat incredible journey, it finally arrives.

This is more good news, even if she has still not received the letter promised by CAF.

More good news in the evening: Marie-Madeleine had applied to be part of the "Guard of Honour" of the Olympic Torchbearers in the municipality, and she was selected.

All the credit goes to her: she had written her candidacy text, and I had only intervened to "give it a makeover."

Imagine her joy: she jumps up like a goat and wants to announce it to the whole world!

D123 (+3 days)

The envelope and the CAF forms have arrived safely. They are asking for, among other things, a collection of copies of documents... that we have already addressed in the SASPA application! But as I had anticipated the process, we have many of the necessary elements, and I have few copies to make.

On the other hand, they ask for a certificate from the landlord in a form that we must send to him, and we can only wait for the goodwill of the landlord.

D126 (+3 days)

Still nothing from the landlord... He lets us know by text message that, on vacation, he does not have a wifi connection or a printer or scan allowing him to answer us.

Forced to wait some longer...

D129 (+3 days)

That's it, we have received the certificate from the landlord. The CAF file is complete, and after a few dozen more photocopies, I close the envelope, and we will post it to-gether. Search, scan, print, send!

A new wait begins...

D142 (+13 days)

There is no news from CAF or the slightest acknowledge-ment of receipt...

A rumour is circulating today in associative circles: "for-eigners who wish to become French must hurry up to pre-pare their files."

What for? How? The proximity of elections raises fears of the rise of the far right, once again, and the disappearance of integration measures. It is impossible to follow the trail and understand the real meaning of the message, but it seems serious.

We thought we still had some time, but we took out the lists to be provided, and the photocopier was back in service.

On the same day, an email from the departmental com-mittee of the Olympics: the Parisian committee asked for "Madeleine's nationality."

We respond immediately, but this adds to our concern: the speeches of the Minister of the Interior all revolve around the police investigations carried out on all the participants in the Olympics, but also on the guests, and associated peo-ple...

Big Brother is on the march!

J143

Naturalization file? The administrative hassle begins again. Have you ever searched for the "P237 tax status slip"?

Sorry: the "Bordereau", with a capital "B"...

Mary Magdalene does not have a "personal account" on the tax website... I try to create it for him, but there is a lack of some number that is impossible to obtain... without a personal digital account. I'm going around in circles once again.

Second attempt: make a direct appointment with the tax authorities.
It's impossible online, without a secure account...
"Thus fon-fon-fon the little puppets... »

Third attempt: call! None of the numbers provided work to obtain information. The machines systematically refer us to the national site – déjà vu! – or even send us away... There is no possibility to ask different questions other than "the level" or "why" of our personal taxes.

Fourth attempt: go to the site... Too late! The services are open four days a week, and only in the morning...
Bad luck, by the time the first three actions were launched, it was noon, and the public accesses were closed until Tuesday. As it is Friday, we will lose another four days for a possible contact.

What time and energy wasted in fruitless steps! "Simplify," they said, "simplify!"
"So fon-fon-fon, three little tricks, and then they're gone!"

D146 (+3 days)
Letter from the CAF to Mary Magdalene, which refers her to the national website and her personal space!
Does this mean that she now has an account?
Half an hour struggle to log in and secure the account, but it works! "Miracle," but notice of "taking charge of (her) request."
And the wait continues...
As a result, I forgot to call the tax authorities for this damn "Bordereau P237"... That will be for tomorrow.

J147
Call the tax service. This is the generic phone number, since the local centers are still not answering.

After a quarter of an hour, I managed to find a – adorable – Parisian interlocutor who, in five minutes, told me to send our request to the local centres: delay, one week. We express our warm thanks to him!
Be continued...

J148

Contact with a local training center so that Marie-Madeleine can register for the TCF[54], a certificate that is mandatory for her application for naturalization to be considered. But the prices of this center are prohibitive: €500 for three hours of training! The passage of the certificate is 170€.
Other centres do not prepare, but pass on: the price of the passage is 170€... to be paid in cash...
As the naturalization application is accompanied by an "electronic" tax stamp of €55, this makes a minimum of €225 to be found...

J149

Mary Magdalene receives a text message from the tax services telling her that she has a message... on his personal space.

I tried a connection again, but we are still missing a "call code," unknown and inaccessible without access... to his personal space. I resign myself to calling.
The local numbers don't answer, but by typing a little at random from the departmental management, I get a box that tells me the address of the customer reception. After the urban riots of 2023, the various local tax services have been somewhat "shaken up" and are reduced to a single reception[55].
It is eleven o'clock: in a hurry, we take the car to try to make direct contact.

---

[54] Test of Knowledge of French. Evaluation of the applicant's level of French, with an oral exam on questions of history, values of the Republic, but also personal involvement, and a written exam on a computer to assess the level of proficiency in the mouse and office software.

[55] The new premises will be inaugurated in May 2024.

Arrived at 11.10. There are about twenty people waiting, but the security guard gives us a number: "693". We are the last: "Afterwards, come back tomorrow, I can't guarantee you a number. The receptions close at noon!"

Waiting in the street, behind a barrier, standing. It's cold, but beautiful, fortunately.

11.40: We can finally enter. There are only two information desks, and one secure payment desk. In fact, it is insufficient to accommodate the crowd of applicants.

And a dozen people are already waiting on a series of chairs, quite uncomfortable.

This is how a game of "musical chairs" begins: the security guard places us on a specific chair.

We are at the end of the line, and each time we go to the counter, he makes all the users move. The ticket is useless: it is the person who passes on chair number "one" who has the right to access the Grail...

It is 12:45 p.m. when we reach the ticket office, and the young woman who receives us is exhausted. But she keeps smiling and her efficiency: in less than fifteen minutes, she pulls out the long-awaited form and the activation codes for Mary Magdalene's personal space.
We thank her warmly.

The administrative file is complete: the TCF still has to be passed, and the electronic tax stamp has to be purchased. Back home, we celebrate this small victory with a well-deserved aperitif!

AND THE WAIT CONTINUES...

Day 150 (5th month)
We got a registration appointment with a local organization close to my home, which administers the TCF. I remain doubtful about the "170€ payable in cash," but as all organizations ask for the same thing, I guess it's a common rule.

Nothing is free in this story: test preparation documents exist, from €10 to €30. I find one that seems serious to me, for about twenty euros, and download it to my computer before printing it.

Once again, the "digital barrier" plays its role of selection as the social barrier of the cost of all these successive operations.

Lamentable, inhumane, and useless procedures: How many potential quality candidates have been eliminated before they have even been able to apply? How many would-be terrorists, financed by drug money, have been able to overcome the obstacle without lifting a finger?

In the meantime, our senators vote for an increase in their "allowances" of €300...

"Eat brioche, if you have no bread!": a revolution was born from this apocryphal phrase[56] attributed to Marie-Antoinette, the elite in those bygone times... Nothing has changed since then, and the well-off are still the first to be served, while students and the "people", now renamed "the last in line", queue in the "restaurants of the heart" to survive.

Keeping hope alive!

D159 (+9 days)

We are received in the training organization by a very courteous, respectful, and very professional woman.

She explains the TCF mechanism to us, makes us sign various papers, pay the 170 euros, and we make an appointment for the test itself, two and a half months later.

Marie-Madeleine could have taken the TCF within the week, but I wanted her to prepare for it. A multiple-choice question[57], for example, is not a trivial method of control. And Mary Magdalene never had one. The rules of the game for a national "test" of this kind are complex and have nothing to do with "real life." She still has a lot to learn...

---

[56] "A quote of dubious origin", a "fake news" probably invented by a polemicist of the time, but that everyone still remembers two and a half centuries later...

[57] Multiple Choice Quiz

Each "failure" is an opportunity for her to bounce back: she becomes aware of the issues, finds solutions, and immediately gets back to work.

I admire her ability to learn and be reassured by her motivation. She will succeed!

D162 (+3 days)

By mail, Marie-Madeleine received a request from the CAF for an RIB[58]. A document was provided a long time ago with the file sent by post.

I connect to the site, and if there is mention of an old, obsolete bank account, the account is blocked with an old address of Madeleine in Paris, dating back almost fifteen years.

I can't change anything. No explanation, of course, just a notice saying, "application closed", but not specifying which one...

We decided to send the bank details by post, with a letter reminding us of our requests following the sending of the SASPA file to RAM Lorraine by the town hall.

Search, scan, print, send!

D170 (+ 8 days)

Still no news from CAF: deep down, I despair!

Mary Magdalene, on the other hand, focuses on preparing for the TCF and is making considerable progress in the tests that we find on the Internet. She learns new words – so do I – and has an effective research approach.

But what Frenchman really knows the "Dates of birth and death of Napoleon 1st"?

When she comes back from the Association, we connect to the CAF website: Yaouh! The account is available.

Unfortunately, the email address given for Mary Magdalene is incorrect... in two places.

I rectify it!

"Normal" that she didn't have any contact...

---

[58] Bank account details.

It is also specified that it has not yet given bank details, while an acknowledgement of receipt "processed file" stipulates that the bank details are registered. One more contradiction...

I rectify and install the bank details "by hand"!

And two other incomprehensible "mistakes"...

I rectify and rectify again...

There is no indication of the processing of our requests, of course...

J171

Notification by email of changes made to Marie-Madeleine's CAF account. Proof that our intervention has borne fruit: his email address is now active.

On her phone, Marie-Madeleine receives an invitation for a handball match from the departmental sports committee, which brings together for the occasion the members of the "Guard of Honour" that will accompany the Olympic flame.

Has Mary Magdalene's candidacy finally been accepted by Parisian security?

No specific contact persons or phone numbers, we send a message back to obtain clarifications. We will not have an answer...

J176 (+5)

Mary Magdalene receives a letter from the MSA Lorraine. This is the first time that this organism has manifested itself with... a request for bank details.

We hurry to send the corresponding mail by post since there is no other way to act. The SASPA file has been registered with the MSA! Thank you, Mr. Mayor, the City Hall, and the CCAS! There is no opinion on the type of decision that may not have been taken yet, but it is already a step forward...

J177

We connect to the CAF website: amazement! Without any notice that her application had been accepted, fifteen days after sending the requested bank details, Marie-Madeleine received housing assistance with a retroactive effect of one month! This covers a small part of his monthly rent! A welcome allowance!

Thank you to the person from the CAF who directed us to this possibility!

I try to get payment certificates from it, but another message tells us that she has not received anything...

The CAF is not without a contradiction, but I assume that there has been a difference in treatment between family benefits and housing assistance in history. Mary Magdalene will have to go to her bank to check.

When in doubt, I make copies of all these elements, out of fear... that they end up disappearing.

In the meantime, we're celebrating: there are no small victories!

ASTERIX, HELP!

J178

Mary Magdalene goes to her bank to check the reality of the transfer: there is nothing, disappointment!

Rumours were circulating on the Internet of difficulties in processing transfers in the banks: we decided to wait a few more days before trying to contact the CAF by phone.

J179

Mary Magdalene goes back to her bank: the money has been paid! It was just a matter of time...

J180 (6th month)

It has been just six months since we started this administrative marathon. If Mary Magdalene remains positive, I am exhausted and partly angry at "the house that makes you crazy![59] ". In the process, I invented a new acronym: RSIE – Search, Scan, Print, Send!

---

[59] A reference to the "*adventures of Asterix the Gaul*" and more particularly to the 1976 film and the album "*The 12 Labours of Asterix*"! The inventor of the "*P237 Slip*" of the tax services must have been inspired by the "*A38 pass*" of Goscinny and Uderzo.

A balance sheet is beginning to emerge, but it is far from being confirmed. Patience!

DISMISSED!

J182 (+2)

Mary Magdalene has received a letter from the MSA: her application for SASPA has been refused. We were dismissed.

The letter is not clear and refers her to an ASPA application (already refused by the CNAV) and a contact with the Pension Insurance and its complementary insurance companies, for a few points recorded for a few years, we don't know how.
Blow to morale... SASPA was a last step, but it still took us six months of our lives...

J184 (+2)

I write letters to the Pension Insurance, the CAF and Agirc-ARRCO, with a copy of the MSA's opinion. Little hope, but that's all we have left.

J185

Mary Magdalene receives an invitation to a gathering of the members of the Olympic "Guard of Honour." This seems to confirm that his application has been accepted... Or was it not refused...

J185

She has regained the morale of a winner: this participation in the "Haie d'Honneur" excites her, and she can't wait to be there. The flame will pass through Évry at the end of July, and we are blocking the day that will be dedicated to it.

D207 (+12 days)

Marie-Madeleine receives a call from the CNAV asking her... a bank account and warning her that she will receive a letter in about ten days.

In his mailbox, a letter, but from Agirc-Arrco, is the sup-plementary fund, which asks him, in addition to new bank details, for a mountain of documents including the birth cer-tificates of his children... Here we go again for a little mara-thon tour!
RSIE – Search, Scan, Print, Send!

She will not receive an "energy check" this year, for rea-sons that seem obscure to me, but it is impossible to protest, or at least, too complicated...

As part of the good news, an invitation from the depart-ment confirms that Mary Magdalene will be part of the "Guard of Honour" of torch smugglers. The "chaperones," like me, are also invited. In addition, we will be treated to a superb handball match and a visit to the VIP area[60]. She ra-diates!

J211 (+ 4 days – 7th month)
An evening of pleasure: the "Haie d'Hon-  *neur" meets in Massy (91) at the "Pierre de Coubertin" stadium. The official "Paris 2024" jerseys have not arrived, and replaced by jer-seys from the department, the organization is a little overwhelmed, but the good mood is general, the match exciting and the buffet friendly. Mary Magdalene is happy, radiant: she laughs, sings, applauds, and thanks everyone, politicians, and sportsmen alike. The Olympic calendar is taking shape, with outings in Paris dur-ing the games.*

D214 (+3 days)
Receipt of the Health Insurance file: lines of entry and dozens of copies of additional documents to be provided, not to mention a bank detail... Probably for nothing, but we are sticking to it once again...
RSIE – Search, Scan, Print, Send!

---

[60] Very Important Person.

J225 (+11 days)

A message from the government, published on "La lettre du Service-Public.fr," announces that a "complaint desk" concerning the 2024 energy voucher will be opened in two months. Mary Magdalene is probably not the only one who has not received this aid this year. We are setting a date.

Message from Agirc-ARCCO, which, ten days after the file was sent, "acknowledges receipt of (your) mail before being taken care of by an advisor." In short: ten days to open the envelope... There is no news of our other different requests.

A moment of emotion: Marika, Marie-Madeleine's second daughter, calls him live from the Congo. She can see, furtively, because the video link is disastrous, Jean-Pierre, her little brother, whom she had not seen for more than fifty years. The book has shaken everyone, and his children are looking for their roots.

D234 (+9 days)

Marie-Madeleine passes her TCF in a few days and becomes feverish... She knows that she has made great progress, but she also knows what she still has to learn. His fears are awakened...

She received an email this evening from the "Olympic and Paralympic Games" team of the Departmental Council, which confirmed her registration for the "Haie d'Honneur" which will accompany the Flame in the department. "Paris 2024 will not send you confirmation," but "we expect you at the end of July." Jubilation and big smiles!

D236 (+2 days)

Here, we are almost eight months into administrative procedures for aid, and still no concrete response to our requests. Neither letters nor emails nor phone calls. It's not far from desperate!

Marie-Madeleine is now taking her TCF: she is stressed, but not as much as I could have imagined. She is confident, open to the unknown and the unexpected. She found the right methods for analyzing requests and constructing responses. She has also regained the dexterity of her youth, with a ten-finger keystroke.

She's ready!

I accompany her to the training center, and I retreat cautiously: I am as stressed as she is, and I don't want to "contaminate" her.

I put the champagne in the fridge: whatever the result, I'm launching the publication of this book tonight, and we're going to celebrate... If she passes her test, it is the start of the naturalization process. If she doesn't succeed, she will prepare it again.

The book? It took him nine months to grow and develop. The time of a birth... virtual. We can't wait to hold it in our hands, smell it, appreciate its texture, and see the readers' reaction.

The first event where we will present it to the public will form a kind of loop: it will be organized in a fortnight by Alexandra Lion, UNESCO Learning City Officer, who had largely contributed to the organization of the "Grand Bazaar of Knowledge". You know, where for the first time we crossed paths, without seeing each other, Mary Magdalene, and I...

It's time: I'm going to get her... It's all over...

Mary Magdalene under the portrait of Simone Veil
© Photo NK 2024 Marie-Madeleine Kabange Ngoie

Mary Magdalene and Alain at a book fair
© 2023 Alain Avanthey

EPILOGUE... TEMPORARY!

RSIE – Hundreds of hours, hundreds of scans and copies, a dozen prints cartridges, dozens of stamps... What for?

The adventure of this book ends here because publication is imminent. But the adventure of life will continue, with the guard of honor of the Olympic torchbearers, the requests for help and retirement, and above all, the series of trials that remain to be faced for Mary Magdalene to become French.
But this is the story of the coming months, a new legend to tell, perhaps...

In conclusion? What more can we say than we have not said?
I would like to quote Jean Jaurès "in the end"[61]:
"I will not bend. I will not go away in silence. I will not submit. I won't look back. I will not comply. I won't go to bed. I will not be silent. Courage is to seek the truth, and to tell it, it is not to submit to the law of triumphant lies."

Good luck to you, readers, may the story of Mary Magdalene inspire you and nourish your self-confidence!

---

[61] French politician born in 1859 and assassinated in 1914.

Alain Avanthey publishes his 28th book with this book.

Management specialist, consultant trainer and certified professional coach, he has been publishing since 1990 and his first novels since 2001.

Of the novel, he often specifies: "a writer cannot remain neutral in the struggles that are taking place for peace, freedom and democracy."

So, "Where have you been? I've been waiting for you! is "a biography totally imbued with the spirit of our time."

And he adds: "This book will undoubtedly make many people cringe, and I designed it to tell the reality: I assume! But no matter the grumpy and annoying ones, it's a life story, a positive story, made to help! ».

Marie-Madeleine and Alain at the 1st Independent
Book Fair (SLI) in Évry (91000 – France) in January 2024
© 2024 Alain Avanthey

Mary Magdalene (72 years old)
© 2024 Alain Avanthev

Mary Magdalene (72 years old)
© 2024 Alain Avanthey

Mary Magdalene in 2024 © Alain Avanthey

Mary Magdalene in 2025 © Alain Avanthey

Mary Magdalene in 2025 © Alain Avanthey

Mary Magdalene in 2025 © Alain Avanthey

Mary Magdalene in 2025 © Alain Avanthey

Mary Magdalene in 2025 © Alain Avanthey

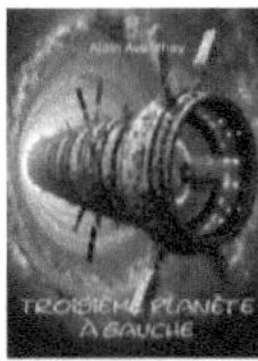

**SF
2025**

Alain Avanthey
Bibliographie romanesque
Des univers littéraires
fascinants

Merci à mes lectrices
et à mes lecteurs !
Merci de partager, vous êtes
ma seule publicité
Suivez le QR Code et
retrouvez ma page auteur
sur Amazon.fr

**Biographie
2024**

**DYSTOPIE
2023**

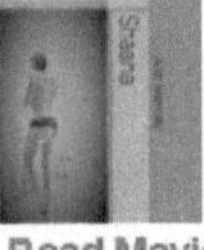

**Conte
écologique
2022**

**DYSTOPIE
2021**

**Road Movie
Érotisme
2020**

POÉSIE - RAP
« Ami, ma poésie… » 4 livrets – 2020

SAGA HISTORIQUE
Parfums d'Avant-Guerres 5 tomes – Romans - 2019 - 2020

FANTASTIQUE
Le Passeur du Gois - La trilogie de Noirmoutier
Romans - 2015

2007   2001
Romans - Épuisé
Commande à l'auteur

Retrouvez les livres d'Alain Avanthey sur www.Amazon.

En fonction de chaque pays, trouvez le site Amazon le plus proche pour commander les livres en format papier.

En format électronique, vous pouvez utiliser le QR Code suivant qui vous conduira sur le site français où vous pourrez les télécharger

///////////////////////////

Find Alain Avanthey's books on www.Amazon.

Depending on each country, find the nearest Amazon site to order the books in paper format.

In electronic format, you can use the following QR Code which will take you to the French website where you can download them